The author is an experienced Home Economics teacher, researcher, and educator with specialised expertise in the field. With extensive experience in professional development for teachers and educators -both nationally and internationally - as well as leadership in an ongoing research project, the author provides well-grounded insights into the demands of teaching. Additionally, as the coordinator of national digital network meetings for professional development through Sveriges Lärare, Sweden's Teachers' Union, the author ensures that the content remains relevant and applicable to today's educational landscape.

The author's collaboration with European higher education institutions contributes to a unique understanding of how educational systems and subject development can be optimised both practically and strategically. Her international engagement includes serving as president of the European Association for Home Economics (EAHE) and vice president for Europe within the International Federation for Home Economics (IFHE). Furthermore, her role as an expert in the Swedish National Agency for Education's monitoring group for Home Economics studies further strengthens the book's relevance.

Legal Framework for Home Economics Education

Foundations for High-Quality Teaching and Learning

Illustration: Elina Larsson/Artelinas.

Publisher: BoD · Books on Demand, Östermalmstorg 1, 114 42 Stockholm, Sverige, bod@bod.se
Printing: Libri Plureos GmbH, Friedensallee 273, 22763 Hamburg, Germany

ISBN: 978-91-8080-885-9

TABLE OF CONTENTS

Abstract

Home Economics is a multifaceted subject that blends theory and practice, requiring sufficient resources and adaptive teaching strategies. Well-equipped learning environments are essential for high-quality education. Surveys conducted in 2020, 2021, 2022, and 2024, reveal that inadequate facilities hinder equity, safety, and compliance with Lgr22, *The Swedish National Curriculum for Compulsory School 2022*. This book stresses the importance of adhering to both Swedish and European legislation, including the Education Act, the Food Act, and the Work Environment Act, to create a safe and legally compliant learning environment. Since the 1990s, significant changes in EU regulations, national legislation, curricula, building standards, and technology have transformed the educational landscape. However, this evolution has not been thoroughly addressed within the context of Home Economics since the Swedish school reform.

Key factors such as class size, scheduling, and professional development play a crucial role in teaching quality. Additionally, the Education Act's focus on individualized learning and human rights is particularly relevant in Home Economics, where students acquire knowledge in nutrition, personal finance, and sustainable consumption. Local policies, such as public health plans and school meal programs, further influence instruction. Implementing risk assessment and conflict management strategies is essential for ensuring a safe and inclusive environment. The findings highlight that compliance with regulatory frameworks and safety measures is vital for fostering an equitable and high-quality learning environment that equips students with practical life skills and prepares them for active, sustainable citizenship.

This book is part of the trilogy *Framework Factors in Home Economics Education*, specifically *Book I: Legal Framework for Home Economics Education – Foundations for High-Quality Teaching and Learning*. The series also includes *Book II: Material Framework for Home Economics* and *Book III: Structural Framework for Home Economics*.

By offering insights into the Swedish context and aligning with international educational trends, this book aims to support educators, policymakers, and researchers in advancing Home Economics education worldwide.

Keywords: Home Economics, education policy, safety regulations, sustainability, food safety, pedagogical strategies, student well-being, HACCP system, inclusive learning environment.

Preface

Home Economics is a cross-curricular school subject where theory goes hand in hand with practice, integrating knowledge from subjects such as languages, mathematics, chemistry, physics, biology, geography, history, religious education, and social studies into various tasks. Lessons in Home Economics cover multiple subject areas aimed at equipping students with the knowledge and skills needed to manage everyday life responsibly. A key focus is on food and meals, where students learn about nutrition, cooking, food safety, and how to plan, prepare, and serve healthy and balanced meals.

Additionally, consumption and the economy are important areas where students gain knowledge on topics such as personal finance, consumer rights, and making informed choices as consumers; this includes budgeting and money management. Sustainability is also a key part of the curriculum, teaching students about sustainable development, the environmental impact of consumption habits, and ways to reduce their ecological footprint by making environmentally friendly choices in their daily lives. The subject also covers health and well-being, focusing on the relationship between diet, exercise, and overall health, as well as developing habits that promote a healthy lifestyle. Finally, lessons include housing and living conditions, where students learn how to manage a household, including cleaning, doing laundry, and performing basic maintenance tasks. Discussions on different types of housing and their impact on everyday life further enhance their understanding. These areas provide students with a broad understanding of how to handle the practical aspects of life, both at home and as consumers in society.

Teaching within the subject of Home Economics is complex. When planning and organising the teaching, as well as the material and structural framework, teachers should base their approach on the Swedish

National Agency for Education's curriculum for the subject, Lgr22. They must also consider the students' developmental stages and needs, along with guidelines for kitchen work and handling raw materials, focusing on hygiene and safety. In practice, this means that the classroom should be a safe learning environment for both students and teachers, one that facilitates learning in practical kitchen work. It should be equipped with the necessary tools and have enough space to serve prepared meals, conduct both digital and traditional classroom teaching, and ensure workplace safety. Considerations for safety include well-planned and functional household appliances, electricity, water, drainage, ventilation, sound levels, and ergonomics. The space should also have functional surfaces for handling and storing raw materials, as well as designated areas for washing, cleaning, hygiene routines, and other household tasks required for teaching with various types of food.

The resources allocated to the subject through school leadership decisions are influenced by an understanding of the subject's specific nature. The Swedish Committee for Home Economics (SKHV, Svenska Kommittén för Hushållsvetenskap), the Teachers' Union's subject council for Home Economics, and the Teachers' Union's national network for Home Economics teachers have worked to clarify and improve the practical conditions of the subject (Hjälmeskog, 2006; Svenska Kommittén för Hushållsvetenskap, 2013). They aim to highlight the subject's versatility and the knowledge areas that benefit students' overall development, as well as the everyday knowledge and skills needed to function as responsible members of society. This includes knowledge that teaches students to become well-functioning consumers. However, survey studies conducted in collaboration with the Teachers' Union in 2020 (N=368), 2021 (N=179), 2022 (N=328), and 2024 (N=372) indicate that these efforts have not led to improved results. Instead, the situation seems to have worsened in recent years.

Purpose of the Book: Part I of the Series

The purpose of this first part in a *trilogy Framework Factors in Home Economics Education,* is to identify and analyse the legal framework conditions that influence learning in the school subject of Home Economics. It examines how these factors affect the teaching of the subject and how pedagogy can be aligned with the requirements of the new curriculum for compulsory schools, Lgr22, as well as other mandatory school forms, including Lspec22, (the curriculum for special school), Lgra22 (the curriculum for adult education), and Lsam22 (the curriculum for Sami school). The goal is to provide an overview of the subject and its framework conditions in relation to key legislation, such as the Education Act, the Work Environment Act, food legislation, the Environmental Code, and the relevant EU regulations. This book will be followed by the other parts of the trilogy *Framework Factors in Home Economics Education:* Book II *Material Framework for Home Economics.and Book III, Structural Framework for Home Economics.*

In this book, the term Home Economics Education is used in the title to stress the broader pedagogical and didactic aspects of the subject, including its legal foundations, curriculum development, and teaching strategies. When discussing the Swedish school subject, both Home Economics Studies and Home Economics are used. The term Home Economics Studies serves as a term for the school subject, as it ensures clarity, consistency, and broad applicability in a European and international context. It is widely recognised in academic and policy discussions, providing a standardised reference for subjects related to nutrition, consumer education, sustainability, personal finance, and household management. Aligning with international research and institutions like UNESCO and the International Federation for Home Economics (IFHE) allows for better collaboration and knowledge exchange. Additionally, this term supports alignment with European educational frameworks and policy development. Since different countries refer to similar subjects by various names, Home Economics Studies serves as a neutral and inclusive term that is easily understood across linguistic and cultural boundaries.

This book does not follow a traditional report format or focus on specific course content. Instead, it highlights teachers' experiences and needs, examines the current state of framework conditions, and offers optimal solutions based on research and proven practice.

Material and Method

The material for this book is based on four qualitative survey studies conducted between 2020 and 2024 for the national network of the Swedish Teachers' Union for Home Economics teachers. These surveys aimed to identify and summarise the fundamental framework conditions of the subject, gain insight into how working conditions vary across different regions, and understand how these variations affect learning.

Another key objective was to map the underlying issues behind teachers' recurring discussions on inadequate framework conditions and to collect their individual perspectives on daily work experiences. The sample consisted of active Home Economics teachers reached through the Teachers' Union's registry. It was open and non-preselected, ensuring that no participants were excluded. The first survey in 2020 received 368 responses (n=368), the second in 2021 176 responses (n=176), the third in 2023 328 responses (n=328), and the fourth in 2024 372 responses (n=372). By distributing the survey through Sveriges Lärare (formerly the Swedish Teachers' Union), with its large and specialised membership base, the likelihood of reaching a broad and relevant group of experienced and engaged Home Economics teachers was significantly increased.

Data collection was conducted through a survey comprising multiple-choice and open-ended questions, divided into five key categories:

1. Teacher background and work tasks
2. Material framework conditions
3. Social conditions in the workplace
4. Organisational prerequisites
5. Current issues, work motivation, and future visions

These categories align with the Swedish National Agency for Education's 2003 national evaluation of compulsory schooling, which identified the most critical framework conditions for Home Economics Studies: classroom facilities, equipment, access to teaching materials, subject budgets, student group size, and lesson duration.

The material for this book comes partly from four qualitative survey studies conducted between 2020 and 2024 for the national network of the Swedish Teachers' Union for Home Economics teachers. The purpose of these surveys has been to understand and summarise the subject's fundamental framework factors, to gain insight into how working conditions vary in different parts of the country, and how this affects learning in the subject.

The multiple-choice questions were mandatory and answered by all teachers. These questions were straightforward, such as: "*Are you qualified in the subject?*" with response options: "*Yes,*" "*No,*" or "*I am currently studying to become a Home Economics teacher.*" The open-ended questions, on the other hand, allowed teachers to share their experiences and reflect on their work situation. For example: "*Are your kitchens sufficiently equipped for the work? Explain. If not, why?*" Teachers could choose whether to respond to these questions and reflect on their pedagogical work from different perspectives. In total, the survey contained over 30 open-ended questions, which received between 30 and

370 responses, covering various framework conditions and their impact on teaching according to Lgr22 and individual teaching practices.

The methodological approach is grounded in a constructivist view of learning, which posits that learning is an active and social process where students interpret their observations and integrate new knowledge with their prior experiences, knowledge, and perceptions (Tynjälä, 1999). This approach aligns with process-oriented learning, which is fundamental to Home Economics. In this subject, students' experimentation, problem-solving, critical thinking, and comprehension play a central role in learning. Constructivism is rooted in cognitive psychology, which focuses on internal processes such as thinking, perception, and memory. From this perspective, the teacher's role is to support students' discoveries and insights during knowledge construction while also identifying potential obstacles in the learning process.

This book is the first in a three-part series and examines the relationship between Home Economics studies and relevant legislation, including the Education Act, the Environmental Code, the Work Environment Act, and food legislation. Responses regarding framework conditions have been assessed in light of the new curriculum (Lgr22) and relevant research. A central question explored in this volume is: *Which legal frameworks influence the creation and implementation of high quality and equitable education?*

The next two books in the series will focus on material and structural framework conditions, drawing on teachers' experiences, subject knowledge requirements, and core content (Swedish National Agency for Education, Skolverket, 2023). They will also examine optimal teaching conditions based on practical experiences and proven research. This trilogy does not merely interpret and analyse theoretical guidelines, but also integrates real experiences from Home Economics teachers, ensuring a comprehensive understanding of the factors that shape teaching quality and learning environments.

Additionally, this trilogy presents perspectives on the technical and functional design of Home Economics classrooms, as well as the equipment used. These perspectives are based on teachers' experiences, teaching requirements outlined in governing documents, interpretations of these documents, and research analysis. Since the 1992 school reform, central authorities no longer regulate the design of school facilities. Instead, teaching spaces are planned and built independently, based on each school's individual goals and needs. The purpose of this trilogy is to establish a solid foundation for defining optimal framework conditions and pedagogical environments for Home Economics studies, using the Swedish National Agency for Education's Lgr22 framework and other relevant governing documents as a basis.

The English version of the text further includes additional explanations, such as insights into the Swedish education system and relevant regulatory documents. The aim is to provide a more comprehensive and nuanced understanding of the subject, particularly for readers outside Sweden who may not be familiar with the Swedish context.

About Framework Conditions

Teaching in Home Economics is influenced by various external factors that both enable and restrict instructional practices. These factors, often referred to as "framework conditions," encompass decisions made at the national and municipal levels, such as timetables, lesson duration, financial resources, and access to teaching spaces and equipment. The overarching educational framework is established and governed by various regulatory documents. According to Chapter 2, Section 35 of the Swedish Education Act (Skollagen, 2010:800), schools are required to provide facilities and equipment that facilitate the achievement of educational goals. For high-quality and equitable education, it is essential to have the appropriate materials, equipment, and tools, along with a learning environment tailored to support students in developing practical knowledge.

Material framework conditions partially overlap with structural ones, as national and municipal decisions on timetables, lesson duration, financial resources, and teaching facilities affect the equity of education. The material framework conditions most frequently highlighted in Home Economics align with framework theory, which emerged during the establishment of comprehensive schools in 1962. Dahllöf analysed the issue of differentiation based on the Stockholm Study (Svensson, 1962; Lundgren, 1999; Aléx P. (2002). He demonstrated that the teaching process is shaped by framework conditions, not in a way that determines a specific learning process or outcome, but rather in a way that enables or restricts different teaching processes - and thus, different learning processes.

In Home Economics studies, material and structural conditions - such as the number of lessons offered, the quality and quantity of kitchen equipment, and the school's financial resources - directly influence how teachers can design their instruction. Framework theory suggests that these conditions do not directly determine what is taught or how students learn, but they do set boundaries for what is possible. Framework conditions such as lesson time, implementation of the subject's timetable, group size, and the design and quality of facilities have been shown to influence teaching (De Ron & Feldt, 2013; Beinert et.al., 2021; cf. Sveriges Lärare, 2023). For example, a school with well-equipped kitchens and sufficient lesson time can provide more hands-on cooking practice and in-depth discussions on nutrition, while a school with limited resources may have to focus more on theory or simpler practical exercises.

As a result, framework conditions influence the content and quality of instruction, which in turn affects students' learning and performance in the subject. This book will explore material framework conditions and discuss them in relation to the Finnish Ministry of Education's guidelines on teaching facilities and safety in Home Economics (Anttalainen, Manninen et al., 2014).

List of abbreviations

AFS

AFS (Swedish Work Environment Authority's Provisions) refers to a collection of binding regulations issued by the Swedish Work Environment Authority to ensure a safe and healthy work environment. Each provision is assigned a unique number and year for reference. For example, AFS 2018:4 sets requirements for workplace first aid and crisis support, ensuring that employers are prepared to handle medical emergencies and provide psychological support during crises.

AML

Arbetsmiljölagen (AML) refers to the Swedish Work Environment Act, which sets the legal framework for ensuring a safe and healthy work environment in Sweden. The law covers aspects such as employer responsibilities, employee rights, workplace safety, and measures to prevent work-related injuries and illnesses. It applies to all workplaces and aims to promote a good physical and psychological work environment. The Swedish Work Environment Authority (Arbetsmiljöverket) oversees compliance with the law.

BBR

BBR stands for *Boverkets byggregler*, which translates to the Swedish National Board of Housing, Building, and Planning's Building Regulations. These regulations set requirements for the design and construction of buildings in Sweden, covering areas such as fire safety, accessibility, energy efficiency, ventilation, and structural integrity. The BBR is an essential part of Swedish building law and ensures that buildings meet safety, health, and sustainability standards.

HACCP

Hazard Analysis and Critical Control Points (HACCP) is a systematic food safety management approach used to identify, evaluate, and control potential hazards in food production. It focuses on preventing contamination by monitoring critical points in the process, such as cooking, cooling, and storage. HACCP is widely used in the food industry to ensure food safety and compliance with regulations.

HE

HE is an abbreviation for Home Economics studies, used in this book as a school subject in Sweden.

Lgr22

Lgr22, *Läroplan för grundskolan, förskoleklassen och fritidshemmet*, refers to the Swedish national curriculum for compulsory school, preschool class, and after-school centres, which was updated in 2022. It includes guidelines for teaching, learning objectives, and assessment criteria for students in Sweden. Lgr22 builds on previous versions but places greater emphasis on knowledge requirements, digital competence, sustainability, and democratic values. Lgr11is the national curriculum before Lgr22.

MSB

The Swedish Civil Contingencies Agency (MSB) is a government agency responsible for strengthening Sweden's ability to prevent, manage, and respond to crises, disasters, and security threats. MSB works with crisis preparedness, civil defence, cybersecurity, and disaster response, both nationally and internationally. The agency plays a key role in coordinating efforts during major incidents, such as wildfires, pandemics, and cyber threats. It also provides guidelines, training, and information to authorities, businesses, and the public, including the well-known brochure "*If Crisis or War Comes.*"

NNR 2023

The Nordic Nutrition Recommendations, *Nordiska närings-rekommendationer*, (NNR 2023) represent the most up-to-date and thorough review of research on diet and health. They outline eating habits that support both short- and long-term well-being and offer guidance on energy and nutrient intake. For the first time, NNR 2023 also takes into account the environmental and climate effects of food choices. These recommendations will form the basis for future dietary guidelines in Sweden and other Nordic countries.

Prop.

Prop. is an abbreviation for proposition, and it refers to a Swedish government bill. For example, the format "2009/10:165" indicates the bill number (165) from the 2009/2010 parliamentary session. If a page number is included, such as (2009/10:165, 872), it refers to a specific page within the bill.

SLVFS

Regulations issued by the National Food Agency (Statens livsmedelsverks författningssamling) are legally binding rules established by the Swedish National Food Agency (Livsmedelsverket) to ensure food safety, hygiene, and consumer protection in Sweden. These regulations cover areas such as food production, labelling, additives, contaminants, and drinking water quality. SLVFS regulations align with EU food legislation but may include additional national requirements. They apply to food producers, retailers, restaurants, and other businesses handling food. The agency regularly updates these rules to reflect new scientific findings and emerging risks.

SFS

The Swedish Code of Statutes is the official collection of all laws and regulations issued by the Swedish government and parliament. Each law or regulation is assigned a unique SFS number, indicating the year and order of publication. For example, the Swedish Environmental Code (Miljöbalken) is designated as 1998:808.

The Validity, Reliability, and Ethical Aspects

The four qualitative survey studies conducted between 2020 and 2024 were answered by 368, 176, 328, and 372 active Home Economics teachers from across Sweden. Approximately 85% of the respondents had worked as Home Economics teachers for more than three years, making their insights reliable and well-informed. The majority were qualified teachers in Home Economics or related fields, such as restaurant and bakery education. Only a small number were unqualified teachers or in the process of becoming certified in the subject.

Although the study is qualitative, the survey included both multiple-choice and open-ended questions, allowing for both qualitative and quantitative analysis methods. The multiple-choice responses were analysed numerically and presented in percentages and figures, while the open-ended responses underwent systematic thematic categorisation and content interpretation. The quality assessment of data processing, analysis, and interpretation was conducted self-critically (Malterud, 1998; Repstad, 2007). To enhance reliability and generalisability, the subject area was carefully examined, and the results were compared with previous research findings and a Finnish model for material framework factors in Home Economics education.

The study adhered to ethical research principles (Swedish Research Council, 2002), following the four aspects of individual protection requirements: information, consent, confidentiality, and usage. Participation was voluntary, and all responses were anonymous. Participants were informed about the study's purpose, and all data was stored and reported in a manner that prevents individual identification. In accordance with the usage requirement, all collected data will be used solely for research purposes.

An inspiring image of a traditional HE classroom in a renovated 1960s school building.
The room features high ceilings and a simple, open floor plan,
offering ample space for movement within the eight student kitchens
By E. Larsson, created using a graphic design program and IKEA's planning tool.

1. The purpose of Home Economics Studies according to Lgr22, Methods and Approaches, as well as the Subject's Core Content.

The structure of Home Economics Studies education is primarily shaped by the curriculum established by educational authorities, which defines the skills, knowledge, and competencies that students are expected to acquire.

When planning and organising instruction, as well as considering the material and structural framework of the subject, the Swedish National Agency for Education's curriculum, Lgr22, should serve as the primary foundation. Additionally, factors such as students' developmental stages and needs, as well as hygiene and safety guidelines for kitchen work and raw material handling, must be taken into account. In practice, this means that the learning environment must be safe and well structured for both students and teachers. It should facilitate practical kitchen work, be equipped with appropriate tools and appliances, and provide sufficient space for both meal consumption and digital or traditional classroom instruction.

Furthermore, the teaching space must be designed with workplace safety in mind. This includes well-planned and properly functioning household appliances, as well as safe and efficient systems for electricity, water, drainage, ventilation, and noise reduction. Ergonomic considerations are also crucial to ensure a comfortable and functional workspace. The room should feature adequate surfaces for raw material handling, storage, washing, cleaning, and hygiene routines, along with facilities for other household-related tasks essential to teaching with various food products.

This chapter is divided as follows:

1.1. The Purpose of Home Economics Education

1.2. Perspectives on Knowledge, Methods, and Approaches in Home Economics

1.2.1. View of Knowledge
The subject's history has shaped its view of Knowledge
Curriculum and the Development of the Subject's Knowledge Perspective
Epistemological Perspectives in Pedagogy

1.2.2. Methods

1.2.3. Working Approaches

1.3. The Subject's Core Content

Food and Cooking

Personal Finance and Consumer Awareness

Lifestyle Habits

Core Content

1.4. Assessment Criteria and Lesson Planning in Home Economics Studies

Assessment Criteria and Student Progression

Incorporating the Central Content into Lesson Planning

Collaborative and Social Learning

Ensuring Cognitive Challenge for All Learners

Practical Learning Tasks That Integrate Theory and Practice

Group Discussions for Shared Learning

1.5. Minimum Number of Guaranteed Instructional Hours for Hone Economics Studies

1.1. The purpose of Home Economics studies

Teaching in Home Economics studies is complex. The subject encompasses all aspects of everyday life, and its core content aligns with most of the overarching goals and guidelines in the Swedish National Agency for Education's curriculum for compulsory schools, Lgr22 (Skolverket 2022, 43):

- The ability to use mathematical thinking for further studies and in everyday life.
- The ability to apply knowledge from the natural sciences, technology, social sciences, humanities, and the arts in further studies, social life, and daily life.
- The ability to solve problems and translate ideas into action in a creative and responsible manner.
- The ability to use both digital and other tools and media for knowledge-seeking, information processing, problem-solving, creation, communication, and learning.
- The ability to think critically and independently formulate positions based on knowledge and ethical considerations.
- The ability to learn, explore, and work both independently and collaboratively while having confidence in one's own abilities.
- Knowledge of societal laws and norms, human rights, and democratic values in school and society.
- Knowledge of the conditions for a good environment and sustainable development, as well as an understanding of how one's lifestyle choices impact health, the environment, and society.

According to the Swedish National Agency for Education (Skolverket), the purpose of the subject is that

---

students develop knowledge and interest in work, economy, and consumer choices in the home. Through a process where thought, sensory experience, and action interact, students should have the opportunity to develop knowledge related to food and meals.

Teaching should thereby contribute to students developing their initiative and creativity in cooking, meal preparation, and other household tasks.

Skolverket 2022, 43

Through teaching in Home Economics studies, the goal is for students to develop an awareness of the consequences their household choices may have on health, well-being, and shared resources. The instruction aims to teach students how their decisions and choices, particularly in relation to household activities and consumption, can influence various aspects of their lives and society as a whole. It is about promoting a conscious and sustainable lifestyle by understanding the long-term effects of their actions on an individual level, a societal level, and the environment.

Students are expected to become informed consumers and household managers, capable of making well-founded decisions that take these different factors into account. The teaching should provide students with the tools and knowledge to make conscious choices in their daily lives. It involves developing an awareness of how their choices affect themselves, their community, and the environment, and how they can act in a sustainable and responsible manner. With these diverse skills, students will ideally feel empowered and confident both as consumers and as members of society.

In practice, students should learn about:

- **Cooking and Everyday Skills:**
  Students should be able to manage various daily situations, such as cooking, doing laundry, and cleaning. They should develop the ability to plan and prepare meals for different needs and contexts, as well as handle other practical household tasks. Additionally, they should understand the importance of time management and organisation.

- **Healthy Eating Habits:**
  Students should receive instruction on nutrition and how food choices impact health, including meal planning and preparation of balanced meals. They should also become aware of food quality and the origins of ingredients.

- **Health and Well-being:**
  A broad perspective on physical, mental, and emotional health should be provided, emphasising the importance of balancing work and leisure time.

- **Sustainable Consumption:**
  Students should be able to discuss the environmental impact of various products and packaging and choose eco-friendly and sustainable alternatives when shopping. They should acquire basic knowledge of recycling and waste management.

- **Personal Finance Skills:**
  Students should gain fundamental knowledge in personal finance, including budgeting and saving. The instruction should help them develop an understanding of the conditions of consumption, as well as payment methods, saving, credit, and loans. This will enable them to make informed financial choices

and handle different consumer-related challenges while understanding the consequences of their financial decisions.

- **Social and Relational Aspects:**
  Discussions should take place about how family roles and relationships influence household decisions and responsibilities. Students should develop communication skills to handle conflicts and collaborate effectively.

- **Societal Impact:**
  Students should reflect on how individual choices influence society and global issues such as justice and sustainability. The teaching should promote understanding of norms, gender equality, and division of labour within the household. Additionally, students should gain knowledge about cultural variations and traditions in different households.

1.2. Perspectives on Knowledge, Methods, and Approaches in Home Economics

1.2.1. View on Knowledge

The Subject's History Has Shaped Its Perspective on Knowledge

The teaching of Home Economics Studies in Sweden has a long history. In the late 19th century, various social issues, particularly those related to household management and the role of the housewife, gained attention. These concerns were linked to broader societal transformations, including industrialisation, urbanisation, and shifting family structures (Nordström, 1989). Industrialisation led to significant rural-to-urban migration, as individuals sought employment in factories. The rapid growth of urban populations resulted in overcrowding and a severe housing shortage. Many families lived in small, cramped, and unsanitary conditions, which posed major health risks, both physical and mental, and contributed to the spread of diseases. Overcrowding and inadequate living conditions led to poor hygiene, which in turn increased the prevalence of illnesses such as tuberculosis and other infections (Eriksson, 1998; Svedberg, 2001). Additionally, high child mortality rates were a pressing concern, often linked to substandard living conditions and limited knowledge of childcare and health.

At the end of the 19th century, women's roles in both the household and the workforce became central issues, as the work of housewives and their responsibility for family well-being were considered essential. There was growing apprehension that women entering the workforce would struggle to fulfil their caregiving roles. This concern intensified as more women sought employment in factories, challenging traditional gender roles and altering the division of labour within families and society (Larsson, 2008; 2011).

Despite economic growth during industrialisation, many families - particularly those in the urban working class - continued to live in poverty. Class disparities became increasingly pronounced, with significant differences in living standards between social groups, thereby heightening awareness of the need for social reforms (Aléx, 2002). Alcohol abuse was also perceived as a widespread issue, contributing to family instability, unemployment, and poverty. Women and children were particularly affected by men's excessive drinking, which fuelled the emergence of social reform movements such as the temperance movement. Concerns over moral decline, especially in urban areas, led to increased efforts to promote morality and hygiene through social reforms and educational initiatives.

These social challenges prompted a range of policy interventions, particularly in housing, social welfare, and education, all aimed at improving living conditions in Sweden. Policymakers and educators believed that enhanced household knowledge could help mitigate poverty, which led to the introduction of cooking and domestic economy education in schools (Aléx, 2002; Hjälmeskog, 2006).

"The oldest of these schools is Gothenburg's Practical Household School for Girls, founded in the year 1865. It possesses its own building, bakery, shop, and a crèche, so that the pupils may also acquire knowledge in the care of children. The course is free of charge and extends over the span of two years.

Amongst other such institutions, one may mention Carnegie's Household School in Gothenburg, established in the year 1891 for the daughters of the sugar refinery's labourers, as well as the Practical Household School in Stockholm, founded in the year 1870, intended for the training of maidservants."

Sundbärg 1901, 1001

In the 1870s, theoretical household studies were introduced in Norrköping, and the subject quickly spread to girls' schools and public schools in larger cities, where dedicated school kitchens were established to facilitate instruction (Lärarnas historia, 2024). By 1893, training programs for female teachers in domestic economy were initiated in both Gothenburg and Stockholm. By the turn of the 20th century, the subject had been formalised with its first official curriculum. To support and further develop this new area of education, local associations for school kitchen teachers were established, beginning in Stockholm in 1902 and later expanding to other parts of the country.

In 1906, the Swedish Association of School Kitchen Teachers (Svenska skolkökslärarinnornas förening) was founded to promote the advancement of school kitchens and advocate for teachers' interests. The association organised professional development courses and campaigned for improved school kitchen facilities. In 1948, it became part of the Swedish Vocational Teachers' Union (Svenska Facklärarförbundet), and in 1963, it was renamed the National Association of Home Economics Teachers (Hushållslärarnas riksförening). The association was dissolved in the 1990s when it merged with Sveriges Lärarförbund, the former teachers' union. Its member magazine, originally titled The School Kitchen Teachers' Journal (Skolkökslärarinnornas tidning), was published between 1916 and 1965 before being renamed The Home Economics Teacher (Hushållsläraren), until its discontinuation in 1990.

The historical development of the subject challenges traditional perspectives on household knowledge by rejecting the notion of domestic work as solely a female responsibility. Today, both boys and girls receive instruction in Home Economics, promoting gender equality and a more balanced division of labour in everyday life. The subject aims to equip students with essential life skills, fostering awareness and competence in areas such as sustainable consumption, nutrition, and personal finance. By encouraging critical reflection on consumption patterns and their consequences, Home Economics studies helps students develop informed and responsible decision-making skills. Additionally, the subject provides practical knowledge in kitchen hygiene, food handling, crisis preparedness, and strategies for maintaining a healthy lifestyle, reinforcing its relevance in contemporary education.

Curriculum and the Development of the Subject's Knowledge Perspective

In Home Economics, theory is integrated with practice, drawing on knowledge from multiple disciplines. By combining theoretical understanding of cooking, economics, hygiene, and sustainability with practical skills, students develop a holistic comprehension of the subject and its relevance to their daily lives (Skolverket, 2020; 2022). The subject fosters both personal and practical development, providing opportunities for students to refine their skills while cultivating independence, responsibility, and problem-solving abilities. Additionally, Home Economics encourages a critical and reflective approach to everyday life, prompting students to examine the norms and values that shape their routines and to explore alternative perspectives and behaviours.

The 2022 national curriculum for compulsory schools, Lgr22, builds upon the foundation laid by Lgr11, maintaining and further developing an integrated perspective on knowledge and learning. Home Economics is not limited to practical skills in cooking and household management; it also encompasses nutrition, economics, and sustainable consumption. Lgr22 emphasises the application of knowledge in real-life contexts and the importance of making informed decisions. As in Lgr11, sustainability remains central to the subject, encouraging students to reflect on their consumption habits and their impact on the environment and society. The curriculum highlights responsible resource use, sustainable cooking, and conscious consumption as key elements of Home Economics.

Both Lgr11 and Lgr22 stress the development of students' critical thinking skills and their ability to make well-informed decisions. Lgr22 continues this focus, equipping students with analytical tools to assess information related to food, economics, and consumption. The use of digital tools in teaching is also stressed, requiring students to search for information, utilise digital resources for planning and budgeting, and understand digital consumption patterns. Lgr22 maintains the student-centred approach introduced in Lgr11, expecting students to take an active role in their learning through practical exercises, collaboration, and reflection. This includes both hands-on tasks in the kitchen and discussions on consumption and household economics. The curriculum retains the assessment structure and progression model from Lgr11, with clear grading criteria that support teachers in evaluating students' skills and development. This assessment framework encompasses both practical competencies and the ability to engage in reasoned discussions on household economics and consumption.

Epistemological Perspectives in Pedagogy

According to the Curriculum for Compulsory Schools 2022, Lgr22 (Swedish National Agency for Education, Skolverket 2024), students are expected to engage in active learning by applying and reflecting on their knowledge construction. This fosters a holistic and integrated understanding of the subject. Central to this pedagogical approach is an emphasis on inquiry-based learning, where students develop knowledge through questioning, exploration, and practical application. Consequently, investigative and inquiry-based teaching methods are highlighted as essential for making students' learning visible and providing a meaningful foundation for assessment. This approach is also reflected in the Swedish National Agency for Education's professional development materials for Home Economics teachers, available through the four modules of the Learning Portal (Skolverket, 2024).

Research consistently demonstrates that clear objectives, structured organisation, and careful planning characterise effective teaching (Hattie, 2009; 2014a; 2014b; Swedish Schools Inspectorate, Skolinspektion 2010). Teachers must continuously articulate learning goals, clarify the purpose of various activities, and present content in a structured and coherent manner. Regular assessment of students' understanding, identification of effective learning strategies, and the provision of targeted support are also critical. Furthermore, summarising different instructional segments helps students develop an overarching understanding of the subject. Educational policy documents emphasise the importance of goal-oriented, teacher-led, and structured instruction, ensuring that students receive clear guidance and support in their learning processes.

Home Economics education is fundamentally practice-based, emphasising learning through action by integrating practical activities and real-life scenarios (McGuirk, 2023a; 2023b; Orre, 2005). Rather than relying solely on theoretical knowledge or passive observation, students actively participate in household tasks, cooking, personal finance, and sustainability-related activities. Through engagement in real-world tasks, they apply their knowledge in practice, fostering a deeper understanding of the subject matter. Additionally, this experiential learning approach enables students to learn from their own experiences and mistakes, promoting long-term retention and critical thinking (Andersson, 2014).

The integration of theory and practice is central to Home Economics studies, as students' theoretical knowledge is continuously reinforced through hands-on activities (Andersson, 2014; Svenaeus, 2009). Findings from the National Evaluation of Compulsory School 2003 (NU-03), (*Nationell utvärdering av grundskolan 2003*) indicate that many of the challenges associated with implementing the subject persist today, particularly those related to structural and material framework conditions. Despite curricular revisions, teachers continue to report that the intended pedagogical goals have not been fully realised due to these constraints (survey responses from 2020, 2021, 2022, and 2024). Addressing these challenges is essential for ensuring that Home Economics education effectively equips students with the skills and knowledge necessary for everyday life.

According to the National Evaluation of Compulsory School 2003, student participation and influence had not increased between NU-92 and 2003, and this challenge appears to persist in schools more broadly. However, Home Economics studies is one of the few subjects that inherently highlights student engagement, particularly in problem-solving and learning processes. The subject fosters active student participation in their own learning and knowledge construction through interaction with both the subject matter and their surroundings (cf. Halås & Fuglseth, 2023; Molander, 1996). In this context, Home Economics studies serve as a platform for students to explore and critically examine various aspects of their daily lives, thereby developing essential skills and understanding.

Home Economics studies offer students opportunities to engage with different work methods and learning approaches through practical tasks and reflective practices. By actively participating in cooking, baking, laundry, cleaning, and raw material handling, students not only apply theoretical knowledge but also develop a deeper, experience-based understanding of these processes. Reflection is a key component of the subject, as students are encouraged to analyse and interpret their experiences and learning outcomes (Skolverket, 2022). Through discussions on personal finance, decision-making, and sustainability, students develop their own perspectives on these topics. These interpretations are shaped through collaboration with peers and teachers, as well as engagement with diverse sources and learning resources.

A central component of the constructivist learning approach is that students take an active role in formulating their own questions and seeking answers. Encouraging inquiry and exploration fosters both learning and creativity (cf. Höijer, 2024). The constructivist approach stresses the active construction of knowledge through interaction with both physical and social environments. In Home Economics studies, when students formulate their own questions within the learning process, they engage in deeper learning through active participation. Rather than passively receiving information, they take the initiative in constructing their own knowledge. The formulation of questions indicates that students are reflecting on their learning and attempting to connect new knowledge to prior experiences. This process enables them to bridge knowledge gaps and develop a more comprehensive understanding of the subject (Chin & Osborne, 2008).

The inherently social and contextual nature of learning in Home Economics studies underscores the pivotal role of the teacher in facilitating process-based education. By guiding students and drawing their attention to key aspects of the learning process, teachers help students understand not only how to perform tasks but also why they are important. While teacher expertise is essential for optimal student learning, other factors also influence learning outcomes, including students' proficiency in learning strategies, motivation, confidence, and self-regulation (e.g., Brown et.al. 1983; Derry & Murphy, 1986; Brown 1997; Garner, 1990). Additionally, the teacher's approach to assessment criteria and pedagogical prioritisation significantly shapes learning. Findings from the National Evaluation of Compulsory School 2003 indicate that teachers often place greater emphasis on specific competencies while giving less attention to broader perspectives, such as gender equality and cultural considerations. These findings reflect long-standing prioritisation patterns in education and remain particularly relevant in contemporary discussions on inclusive education and diversity.

A fundamental aspect of teacher competence is the ability to effectively communicate learning objectives and assessment criteria. The gap between teachers' and students' perceptions of learning goals and assessment remains a recurring issue in educational discourse. Clearly articulated objectives and transparent assessment criteria are essential for ensuring that students understand expectations and can work toward achieving them.

Three key elements have been identified as essential for teaching that integrates both knowledge and action: practice and training, discussion and reflection, and personal engagement and participation (Enfield et al., 2007; Molander, 1996). Teachers can foster students' critical thinking by asking varied and thought-provoking questions that challenge assumptions and encourage deeper inquiry. This pedagogical approach is emphasised in the Swedish National Agency for Education's professional development modules for Home Economics studies. In one such module,

Karin Höijer (2024) highlights attention as a crucial component of learning through action. She argues that sustained attention requires continuous practice and structured guidance. By directing students' focus toward the action itself, teachers help them develop a clearer understanding of processes and outcomes. This dynamic interplay between exploration and learning allows students to refine their experiences and perspectives. Furthermore, observing the actions of others can expand and shift students' attention, enhancing their understanding. To facilitate meaningful learning, students require well-defined goals and strategic guidance. Inquiry-based and question-driven teaching methods can provide this necessary structure and focus.

Another central concept emphasised by Höijer (2024) is reflection. Reflection involves stepping back to critically evaluate actions, reconsider past experiences, and contextualise learning within a broader framework. A developing reflective process alternates between direct engagement with a situation and deeper contemplation, enabling students to recognise patterns and make informed adjustments. Learning through doing, combined with active attention, fosters this reflective process. Additionally, students benefit from developing awareness of their own cognitive and behavioural strategies, as these influence their ability to acquire and apply knowledge. The personal orientation system, which comprises an individual's values, habits, strategies, and underlying assumptions, plays a crucial role in shaping both inquiry and reflection. The everyday practices examined in Home Economics studies often intersect with unconscious aspects of this orientation system, making reflection a vital tool for fostering critical awareness and continued knowledge development.

1.2.2. Methods

Cooking methods and techniques play a fundamental role in the constructive learning process of Home Economics studies by providing students with a hands-on, engaging platform to explore and develop their understanding of cooking, food culture, and related topics. Through practical actions such as chopping, slicing, frying, boiling, and baking, students not only acquire specific culinary skills but also develop an understanding of how different ingredients and techniques interact to create various dishes. This experiential learning approach allows students to experiment, reflect, and deepen their knowledge of cooking and food cultures. Mastering these techniques requires both fine and gross motor skills, as well as repetition and practice. The objective is not merely to teach students how to prepare specific dishes (cf. Bohm, 2022) but to equip them with a versatile understanding of various techniques, enabling them to adapt their skills to different everyday situations. Teaching that prioritises meal production over process-oriented learning often results in a goal-driven approach, where emphasis is placed on the sensory qualities of the meal and fitting lessons within time constraints (Gelinder, 2020; Lindblom, 2016).

Teaching cooking methods in Home Economics studies necessitates interaction with the learning environment, making material and structural conditions significant factors in the learning process. The availability of kitchen equipment and materials is crucial - well-equipped kitchen facilities with appropriate tools and ingredients enable students to engage safely and effectively in cooking activities. Access to a variety of utensils, appliances, and fresh ingredients allows for more immersive and realistic learning experiences, facilitating students' exploration of different cooking techniques and recipes.

Furthermore, the physical design and organisation of the classroom play a critical role in the learning process. A well-structured, functional kitchen environment fosters student collaboration, communication, and the ability to follow instructions. An organised layout enhances the teacher's ability to supervise and provide feedback, ensuring that students receive guidance throughout their cooking activities. Additionally, clear safety measures and hygiene routines are essential in culinary education. Implementing well-defined safety and hygiene protocols helps students develop confidence in handling kitchen tools, working with sharp objects and hot surfaces, and maintaining clean and sanitary workstations.

Teaching cooking methods in Home Economics studies also emphasises flexibility and adaptability. A dynamic and responsive learning environment is essential for accommodating students' diverse needs and learning styles. By offering varying levels of challenge and complexity, teachers can differentiate instruction and optimise learning for each student (cf. Lindblom, 2016). Moreover, fostering an environment that encourages student feedback allows for continuous improvement of teaching methods. Students' questions and reflections arise in response to both the physical environment - such as cooking methods and equipment - and the social environment, including interactions with peers and the teacher. Through active engagement with their surroundings, students gain opportunities to experiment, explore, and deepen their understanding of the subject.

Effective practical learning in Home Economics studies requires an ongoing and iterative learning process, where students continuously develop both theoretical and practical knowledge of various work methods. Through hands-on experimentation and active engagement, students construct their own knowledge by integrating new information with prior experiences and understandings. This dynamic process fosters a deeper and more cohesive knowledge base, enabling students to develop their own interpretations and solutions to real-world problems within the subject. By actively participating in problem-solving and decision-making, students gain a more meaningful and applicable understanding of Home Economics studies and its relevance to their daily lives.

Additionally, cooking and baking methods serve as valuable tools for teaching broader skills and concepts. For instance, cooking activities can help students develop an understanding of measurement units, proportions, financial responsibility, and sustainability principles (cf. Skolverket, 2022). By integrating cooking with other subject areas and real-life contexts, educators can create a holistic and interdisciplinary learning environment where students apply and expand their knowledge in meaningful ways. This approach reinforces the practical value of Home Economics studies, preparing students to make informed choices that affect their personal lives and society at large.

An inspirational image of working methods.
Av E. Larsson/Artelinas.

1.2.3. Working Approaches

Home Economics studies is a process-oriented subject, meaning that the emphasis is placed on the work process itself rather than solely on the final result. Learning occurs through active participation in practical activities and reflection on experiences, fostering a deeper understanding of the subject. Instead of merely following a recipe to prepare soup, for example, students explore the various steps involved in the cooking process, the rationale behind ingredient choices, and the impact of different factors on the final outcome. This approach encourages the development of transferable skills and methods that can be applied in a variety of contexts.

A typical Home Economics studies lesson follows a structured sequence, as identified by several researchers. Ingela Bohm describes lessons as commonly moving through different phases, beginning with an establishment phase where expectations are set and preparations are made. This is followed by an introduction in which objectives, concepts, and instructions are presented. The main part of the lesson consists of student work, where theoretical knowledge is applied through hands-on activities. The meal itself becomes a central part of learning, integrating discussions on food culture, sustainability, and nutrition. Finally, lessons conclude with reflection, where students analyse the process, discuss outcomes, and evaluate what they have learned.

In practice, these phases often overlap, particularly between student work and the meal. Students may, for instance, choose to clean their kitchens after eating together, blending different elements of the lesson into a more seamless experience. This flexible and interactive structure supports both independent learning and collaboration, reinforcing the importance of a process-oriented approach in developing essential life skills.

1. **Establishment**
   In this phase, the teacher prepares the classroom and creates a learning environment with both material and theoretical preparations. This may include informing students about the lesson objectives, reviewing rules and routines, and fostering an open and welcoming atmosphere. From a constructivist perspective on the learning process, the teacher can create an interactive and student-driven environment where students' prior knowledge and experiences are considered. Encouraging students to share their previous experiences related to the day's topic and tasks establish a sense of relevance and connection to prior learning.

2. **Introduction**

   Here, the teacher introduces the topic or activity for the lesson, such as the recipe and the various methods that will be used during the work. This may include demonstrating techniques or methods, showing examples, or providing background information about the lesson task. When introducing the day's topic or activity, the teacher can use exploratory questions and problem-based learning to spark students' curiosity and engagement. Instead of merely presenting facts, the teacher can guide students to discover and explore the topic on their own, promoting active learning and knowledge construction.

3. **Student Work**

   During this phase, students have the opportunity to actively engage in practical tasks or exercises related to the subject, such as practicing different methods. This may include cooking, baking, or other household activities where students apply the knowledge they have acquired. During the student work phase, it is important to encourage students' own exploration and experimentation. By allowing students to work in pairs, in groups, and collaborate on practical tasks, they can construct their own understanding and share different perspectives and experiences.

4. **Meal**

   In this phase, students usually get the opportunity to taste or eat what they have prepared during the lesson. This allows them to appreciate and reflect on their work while experiencing the practical consequences of cooking. During the meal phase, encouraging students to reflect on their cooking experience can integrate constructivist learning. The teacher can ask open-ended questions that stimulate students' thinking about the taste, texture, and nutritional content of the food they have prepared. By encouraging students to express their thoughts and opinions, they can develop a deeper understanding of the connection between cooking and health.

5. **Closing**

The closing phase includes summarising and reflecting on what has been learned during the lesson. The teacher can revisit the lesson objectives, ask students to share their thoughts and experiences, and provide feedback and evaluation of their performance. The closing phase can be used to summarise the day's learning and encourage students to reflect on their experiences and insights. The teacher can encourage students to identify what they have learned and how they can apply their knowledge in future situations, promoting long-term learning and understanding.

According to the Swedish National Agency for Education's new modules for the subject, *Module 1: Knowledge Perspective* (Höijer, 2024), there is an emphasis on inquiry-based and question-driven teaching as a way to achieve optimal learning outcomes (Britton & Johansson, 2022; Holmberg et al., 2022). This approach incorporates many elements of constructivist learning, and according to Banchi & Bell's (2008) model, students learn through four different levels by working with analysis and questioning:

1. **"The Confirmation Level"**

This is the first level, where students are provided with a predefined question, method, and expected outcome, helping them reinforce prior knowledge and understand new concepts. The focus here is on allowing students to experience and confirm theories in practice, providing them with a foundational understanding of the subject. Within constructivist pedagogy, this level serves as a fundamental building block that prepares students for more independent learning. It is often used to review previously learned concepts or introduce students to a new method. For example, students may confirm that overcooked pasta loses its firmness by following a given protocol, documenting their results, and then discussing their observations.

2. At **"The Structured Inquiry Level"**
    students are given a theme, a question, and a method, but they are expected to investigate and determine the outcome themselves. This level encourages students to start thinking more critically and explore different possibilities, which is central to constructivism. While students still receive guidance, they are also given the opportunity to make their own discoveries, strengthening their ability to draw conclusions based on their own observations. For example, students might explore what happens to pasta when the cooking time is too long, without being given the answer in advance.

3. At **" The Guided Inquiry Level"**
    students are provided with only a theme and a question from the teacher, and they must independently choose a method to find the answer. This level supports deeper understanding by making students more active participants in their learning process. Within constructivist pedagogy, this is a crucial phase where students begin to take greater responsibility for their own learning, explore different paths to knowledge, and develop their analytical skills. For example, students might investigate the optimal cooking time for pasta.

4. The final level, **"The Open Inquiry Level"**,
    offers maximum independence, where students choose their own topic, formulate questions, determine methods, and conduct the investigation. This promotes a high degree of student autonomy and creativity, aligning with constructivist pedagogy. Here, students take full responsibility for their learning, allowing them

to explore their own interests and questions, which strengthens their ability to work independently and critically analyse their results. For example, they might be tasked with exploring different aspects of pasta or the cooking process.

By applying these four levels, the pedagogy in Home Economics studies supports a gradual shift from teacher-led to student-led learning. Students start by confirming and understanding fundamental concepts before advancing to more independent and creative exploration. This structured progression fosters critical thinking, problem-solving abilities, and a sense of responsibility for their own learning, aligning with the principles of constructivist pedagogy. Through this approach, students gain both theoretical knowledge and practical skills while developing the confidence to apply their learning in real-life situations.

An inspirational image of a traditional HE classroom in a newly built school.
The room features spacious areas, large window sections,
and modern, bright student kitchens.
By E. Larsson, created using a graphics program
and IKEA's planning tool.

1.3. The Subject's Core Content

Teaching in Home Economics education is multifaceted, covering all aspects of daily life while meeting the majority of the Swedish National Agency for Education's (Skolverket) learning objectives in the national curriculum, Lgr22. The curriculum outlines the skills, knowledge, and competencies that should be included in the subject. According to Skolverket (2022), Home Economics education for grades 7–9 should cover three main areas: *Food and Cooking, Personal Finance and*

Consumption, and *Lifestyles*. These core areas are further divided into multiple knowledge components that make up the subject's central content.

The governing documents, including the curriculum and syllabi, provide the foundation for teachers' work in compulsory school. The curriculum defines the school's mission, fundamental values, and overarching goals, while the syllabi outline the purpose, core content, and assessment criteria for each subject. Teachers design their instruction based on these guidelines to ensure that students acquire essential knowledge and skills. Assessment criteria serve to evaluate students' progress and must be interpreted in relation to both the taught content and the intended learning outcomes.

To support teachers in this process, the Swedish National Agency for Education offers resources such as *How to Use the Syllabi* and commentary materials that provide deeper insights into the structure and rationale of the syllabi. This is necessary, as the Swedish Schools Inspectorate's review (Skolinspektionen, 2019) shows that teachers' knowledge of the entire core content of the subject influences how they prioritise when planning and conducting lessons. In many cases, the full core content is not taught; instead, teaching is limited to the parts that each teacher feels most comfortable with. Additionally, other factors, such as resource availability, time for planning, and the school's organisational conditions, also have a significant impact on how well the subject's core content is delivered. The agency underscores the importance of systematically aligning teaching with these governing documents to ensure an equitable education for all students. By understanding and applying the curriculum and syllabi effectively, teachers can adapt their instruction to meet students' needs and fulfil the established educational objectives.

Core Content for Grades 7–9

Food and Cooking

- Cooking for different needs and contexts.
- Properties and uses of food ingredients.
- Selection of ingredients and cooking methods, including baking. Planning, organising, and evaluating the work.
- Creating personalised meals, for example, based on seasonal ingredients and leftovers.
- Instructions and recipes - how to read and follow them, as well as terminology related to cooking.
- Discussions about sensory experiences, such as taste, smell, consistency, and texture in cooking.
- Tools and kitchen equipment used in cooking, and how to use them functionally and safely.
- Hygiene and food safety related to handling, cooking, and storing food.

Personal Finance and Consumption

- Youth personal finance: consumption and financial planning, including budgeting.
- Purchasing on credit, signing subscriptions, borrowing, and saving money.
- The difference between objective consumer information and other influences on consumption choices. Advertising in various forms, including hidden marketing messages.

- Consumer rights and responsibilities: warranties, complaints, right of withdrawal, return policies, and purchases from private individuals, as well as the differences between in-store and online shopping.

Lifestyle Habits

- Composition of varied and balanced meals adapted to individual needs.
- The significance of meals for social bonding and different food traditions.
- Division of household work from a gender equality perspective.
- Resource management: decision-making regarding the selection and use of food and other goods. How production, transportation, and recycling of food and other goods impact human health, economy, and the environment.
- Routines and methods for cleaning and laundry.

Skolverket, 2022 (Lgr22)

Food and Cooking

According to the new curriculum, Lgr22, a key focus in the *Food and Cooking* area is for students to learn how to adapt cooking to different needs and contexts while understanding the properties and uses of food ingredients. They should be able to select appropriate food products and cooking methods, including baking, and develop the ability to plan, organise, and evaluate their work. Additionally, students should learn to create their own meals by using seasonal ingredients and leftovers, follow instructions and recipes, and understand cooking terminology. They should also be able to discuss and analyse sensory experiences related to taste, smell, texture, and consistency in food preparation. A fundamental part of their learning is the safe and functional use of kitchen tools and technical equipment, as well as hygienic food handling, cooking, and storage. In essence, students should develop both practical and theoretical cooking skills to prepare healthy and safe meals suited to various needs and situations.

Personal Finance and Consumer Awareness

The Swedish National Agency for Education also highlights the importance of *Personal Finance and Consumer Awareness* in equipping students with the knowledge needed to manage their financial resources and make informed consumption decisions. Teaching should aim to help students understand financial management, including budgeting and planning for future financial goals. Students should gain knowledge about handling credit, subscriptions, loans, and savings, as well as the risks and benefits associated with different financial products.

The school subject of Home Economics plays a vital role in addressing the alarming gaps in financial literacy and the evolving consumption patterns among young adults (*Young Personal Finance, Ung Privatekonomi*, 2021). Many young people express a strong desire for more personal finance education in schools. According to the Swedish Enforcement Authority, Kronofogden (2022), the median debt among young women doubled between 2011 and 2021, highlighting growing concerns about financial awareness and sustainable consumption. This rise is primarily driven by consumer debt. While the number of indebted young adults aged 18–25 has decreased in Kronofogden's records, the total debt for this age group has increased by 410 million SEK. The Swedish Enforcement Authority is a government agency responsible for debt collection, enforcing court rulings, and ensuring that outstanding debts are settled. It assists individuals and businesses in recovering unpaid payments while also offering support and guidance to those facing financial difficulties. Additionally, Kronofogden works to prevent overindebtedness by promoting financial responsibility and debt management awareness.

Furthermore, Home Economics as a school subject should foster a critical approach to consumption choices, helping students distinguish between factual consumer information and external influences, particularly advertising. Students should also become familiar with their rights and responsibilities as consumers, including warranties, complaints, withdrawal rights, and the differences between in-store and online shopping. Understanding the laws and regulations governing consumer purchases is an essential part of this education.

Lifestyle Habits

Within the framework of *Lifestyle Habits*, it is crucial for students to develop a fundamental understanding of key aspects of health, sustainability, and social responsibility. A central component of this is learning to compose varied and balanced meals tailored to individual nutritional needs while understanding the significance of nutritious choices for a healthy lifestyle. Additionally, students should recognise the role of meals in fostering social connections and appreciate the diversity of food traditions, which can enhance cultural understanding and respect.

The Swedish National Agency for Education emphasises the importance of promoting gender equality in household labour distribution, as this helps prepare students to build fair and equitable relationships in the future. By learning about resource management and understanding how food and consumer choices affect health, the economy, and the environment, students can make more informed and responsible decisions that benefit both themselves and society. Furthermore, acquiring practical knowledge and skills in cleaning and laundry is essential for maintaining personal hygiene and a healthy home environment.

According to the new curriculum, Lgr22, students should be encouraged to apply critical thinking (Skolverket, 2022). Teaching should facilitate this by providing students with repeated opportunities to acquire relevant knowledge, critically evaluate information, question common assumptions, and examine different perspectives. One effective approach is designing tasks that require students to assess various consumption options, analyse advertising messages, and evaluate household cost distributions. Additionally, students should be encouraged to reflect on their own values. Through exercises and discussions, they can examine their personal beliefs and norms in relation to the subject's key areas: food, health, consumption, and economy. Developing awareness of one's own values is essential for making informed choices.

A critical aspect of awareness is the ability to analyse consequences. Students should learn to assess the impact of different choices and actions on both themselves and society. This may include discussing the environmental implications of various consumption habits or reflecting on how financial decisions influence personal and societal economies. According to Skolverket's teaching modules for Home Economics studies, *Module 3: Beyond Normative Teaching* (Hjälmeskog, 2024), the subject plays a vital role in educating the younger generation on how to live healthily and sustainably. Home Economics studies equips students with both practical and theoretical knowledge, enabling them to reflect on and critically examine the norms that shape their daily lives.

These tools encompass various aspects of the subject, aiming to promote a critical and conscious perspective on everyday actions and decisions. To advance sustainable development, profound changes are needed in how we live, communicate, think, feel, and even taste (Böhme et al., 2022; Gerlinder, 2024). The traditional view of humans as separate from nature and others must be reconsidered in favour of an approach that recognises our interconnectedness. It is essential to understand that individual actions impact not only oneself but also the broader community, and students must feel that they are not alone in their efforts toward change. Particularly concerning consumption and lifestyle choices, positive reinforcement from teachers plays a crucial role in encouraging development and creating opportunities for change and progress (Hjälmeskog, 2024).

Core Content

As highlighted in the subject's core content, Home Economics studies also involves ethical considerations, such as resource management within households regarding the selection and use of food and other goods, as well as the impact of production, transportation, and recycling on human health, the economy, and the environment. Research indicates that students' existential questions are often underrepresented in Swedish school education (Sporre, 2022). According to Karin Hjälmeskog (2024) in Skolverket's Module 3, ethical competence is typically highlighted through rational thinking and the ability to argue, with a focus on classic dilemmas offering alternative solutions. This approach risks making lessons feel dull, artificial, and contrived. Instead, teaching should be rooted in students' own perspectives and inquiries. As mentioned earlier regarding the subject's knowledge approach, communication plays a vital role in education (Sporre, 2022), including actively listening to students to make learning meaningful for them.

Often, Home Economics studies teachers divide the subject's content into aspects of health, economy, and environment to better teach resource management in practice: how should students learn to make informed choices regarding food and other goods, and understand how their production, transportation, and recycling impact human health, the economy, and the environment? However, these areas are often interwoven, and for individuals, significant changes in dietary habits affect all these aspects. For the individual student and consumer, a comprehensive dietary transformation inherently involves considerations of health, economy, and the environment.

The subject's core content has a strong connection to the United Nations' Agenda 2030 (UN, 2023) and its sustainability goals, as many of the 17 goals relate to food. Goal 12, which focuses on sustainable consumption and production, is particularly relevant to sustainable food consumption. Goal 12 includes sub-goals such as halving global food waste (12.3) and increasing public awareness of sustainable lifestyles (12.8). Students should gain knowledge on promoting sustainability, for example, through food transformation, which generally requires an increased consumption of plant-based foods and a reduced intake of animal products (Blomhoff et al., 2023; Willet et al., 2019). The Nordic Nutrition Recommendations (NNR) were updated in 2023 based on the latest research on how we should eat for optimal health (Blomhoff et al., 2023).

In Skolverket's teaching module Part 4: *A Taste for Sustainability*, Lolita Gerlinder (2024) highlights the crucial role of taste in our food choices - since we naturally prefer to eat what we find tasty (Belasco, 2008; Højlund, 2020; Schmidt & Mouritsen, 2020). To motivate students to learn about and appreciate diverse tastes, as well as understand different culinary traditions, it is not enough to simply instruct them on what they should eat. It is essential to inspire them to develop new habits. Since new, more environmentally friendly foods are continuously being introduced, students should become familiar with new flavours and potentially adjust their taste preferences to eat both healthily and sustainably (Højlund, 2020).

The school has a dual role:

---

to impart timeless fundamental skills such as reading, writing, and mathematics while also adapting to contemporary challenges and context-specific needs.

The Government Offices of Sweden (2020), SOU 2020:28.

In navigating this balance, the school must both equip individuals with the competencies to become independent and knowledgeable, as well as address and adapt to the prevailing social, cultural, and economic conditions. In other words, the school must not only prepare students for life in general but also provide them with the tools to face and understand the specific challenges of their time and society.

In Home Economics studies, this means that teaching should include both timeless knowledge, such as household management and economics, and be adapted to current issues like sustainability and consumption habits, enabling students to navigate today's society in a competent and informed manner. The Swedish National Agency for Education's (Skolverket) new curriculum also encompasses this essential aspect, emphasising that students should learn to become conscious and active citizens during their schooling. Home Economics studies provides tools to develop students' ability to actively participate in society as informed and responsible citizens. This involves navigating complex issues, making informed decisions, and influencing change. To act as responsible citizens, students need knowledge of empathy and solidarity. This means acquiring fundamental understanding in areas such as justice, sustainability, and global issues, allowing them to develop empathy and solidarity towards other people and societies. Such knowledge fosters greater awareness and engagement in contributing to a fairer and more sustainable world.

The subject of Home Economics studies covers a wide range of topics, making the teacher's role crucial in delivering high-quality education. To effectively navigate the subject's broad content - spanning health, economics, and environmental aspects, which may touch on controversial and emotionally charged topics - teachers need strong expertise across the different domains within Home Economics studies. This includes practical skills, theoretical knowledge of methods and food chemistry, nutrition, personal finance, consumer legislation, and environmental issues. Furthermore, teachers must be prepared to address both their own and their students' emotions, including both positive and negative feelings related to necessary changes for a more sustainable future. Students may need to explore and process emotions that arise when their habits, routines, and aspirations are discussed and potentially questioned. Examining different perspectives and asking "how" and "why" can evoke strong emotions in students (cf. O'Doherty Jensen & Holm, 1999). As a Home Economics studies teacher, it is crucial to acknowledge and engage in discussions about negative emotions, as well as feelings of discomfort or concern, which may manifest in different ways in the classroom (Ojala, 2016).

By learning and applying various tools in Home Economics studies, students gain not only practical skills but also the ability to reflect on and take action in a world shaped by diverse norms and values. This is essential for creating a sustainable and meaningful everyday life, both for themselves and for society as a whole.

1.4. Assessment Criteria and Lesson Planning in Home Economics Studies

This section has been added to provide a broader perspective on the subject's content and its didactics, making it easier to understand. This part is not included in the Swedish version of the book.

In Swedish compulsory school, the assessment criteria for Home Economics studies in Year 9 range from E to A, reflecting students' abilities in meal preparation, household tasks, financial literacy, and sustainability considerations (Skolverket, 2022). Teachers must align their lesson planning with these criteria and the central content of the subject to ensure a structured and equitable learning process.

Assessment Criteria and Student Progression

E (Pass Grade):
The student uses mostly functional methods to plan and prepare meals and manage household tasks. Their evaluation of their working process and its impact on results is simple. They briefly describe factors affecting personal finance and consumer choices and provide a basic evaluation of how household decisions influence health, economy, and the environment.

C (Mid-Level Proficiency):
The student applies functional methods and develops their reasoning about how the work process affects the outcome. Their descriptions of financial and consumer decisions, as well as evaluations of household choices, are more elaborated.

A (High Proficiency):
The student demonstrates highly functional approaches, reflecting a well-developed ability to plan, execute, and assess their work. Their descriptions, evaluations of financial, and consumer choices are in-depth and well reasoned.

Incorporating the Central Content into Lesson Planning

As mentioned before, the central content covers meal preparation and nutrition, including cooking techniques, meal planning, and dietary guidelines. It also explores consumer economics, focusing on budgeting, saving, debt, and consumer rights. Additionally, it addresses sustainability and environmental impact, stressing the reduction of food waste, ethical consumption, and energy use in households (Skolverket, 2022).

When planning lessons, teachers must differentiate instruction to ensure that students at different proficiency levels (E-A) receive appropriate challenges. They should integrate hands-on activities, such as cooking labs and budget planning exercises, to reinforce practical skills. Additionally, teachers need to encourage reflection through discussions and written evaluations, helping students develop their ability to assess their own processes and decision-making. It is crucial for teachers to use real-world examples, such as analysing grocery shopping habits or investigating sustainable food choices, to make learning relevant. By aligning instruction with both the assessment criteria and central content, teachers can guide students toward higher levels of proficiency while ensuring they acquire essential life skills.

From a constructivist perspective, learning is an active process in which students build knowledge through experience, social interaction, and personal reflection. Differentiating instruction in Home Economics studies should emphasise scaffolding, student agency, and collaborative learning to ensure that students at different proficiency levels (E-A) receive meaningful and developmentally appropriate challenges. It is crucial to clearly define the differences between proficiency levels and specify what students need to demonstrate in practice to achieve an A level.

Constructivism emphasises learning by doing, which aligns well with the practical nature of Home Economics. Teachers provide scaffolded instruction in various ways:

- Offering systematic guidance for students at lower grades and the E level while gradually reducing basic support for higher-achieving students, who instead receive tasks that are more challenging.
- Using guided inquiry, where students explore different cooking techniques or budgeting strategies and reflect on their outcomes.
- Encouraging self-directed learning by allowing advanced students to experiment with meal planning, ingredient substitutions, or sustainability projects.

Constructivist learning involves personal meaning making and ownership of learning. Teachers typically allow students to co-create meal plans or household budgets based on their interests and cultural backgrounds. They also provide choice-based tasks, such as selecting recipes of varying complexity or designing their own sustainable consumption projects. Additionally, students are encouraged to engage in self-assessment and reflection, evaluating their work processes and connecting their learning to real-life decision-making.

Collaborative and Social Learning

According to Vygotsky's social constructivism, learning occurs through interaction with more knowledgeable peers. Since Home Economics is a broad subject, students develop different types of competencies and skills -ranging from theoretical knowledge to practical abilities, such as handling various methods, motor skills, seasoning food, and distinguishing between different textures and consistencies. Because of these varied skill sets, students can learn a great deal from one another (Larsson, 2024, Skolverket Modul 2).

Students typically work in pairs, making peer teaching a practical approach. Students at different proficiency levels collaborate, simultaneously developing their own understanding while supporting their classmates. Skolverket encourages the use of group work as a method when appropriate. Group problem-solving activities, such as analysing food waste reduction strategies or comparing grocery budgets based on nutritional value, are commonly used. Additionally, reflective discussions allow students to share their decision-making processes and learn from different perspectives.

Ensuring Cognitive Challenge for All Learners

Differentiation in Home Economics studies does not mean simplifying tasks for some students but rather adjusting the level of challenge. Basic food preparation methods can be used to create A-level dishes when combined with different techniques and when students are able to reflect on their work, including how they explain their results. The ability to adapt in different or problematic situations is also an indicator of a higher proficiency level, as is the ability to explain changes in methods afterward. In general, reflections on each task can vary in depth, ranging from simple cause-and-effect descriptions (E) to critical analysis of interconnected factors (A) (Skolverket, 2022). For example, students might examine how results vary depending on different temperatures and cooking methods or how different techniques can be used to achieve the same outcome. By applying constructivist principles to differentiate instruction, teachers ensure that all students engage actively, construct knowledge at their level, and develop essential problem-solving and critical-thinking skills that prepare them for real-life decision-making in home and consumer contexts.

Practical Learning Tasks That Integrate Theory and Practice

Home Economics studies emphasises active, experiential, and reflective learning, where students construct knowledge through hands-on engagement, personal experiences, and critical thinking. In alignment with constructivist principles, learning is built through active participation rather than passive absorption. By integrating practical activities, reflection, and real-world examples, students gain essential life skills while deepening their understanding of core concepts.

Practical activities such as cooking labs and budget planning exercises provide students with direct experience, reinforcing theoretical knowledge through real-world application. Instead of merely reading about nutrition or food preparation, students learn by doing - actively engaging with the material to develop both procedural and conceptual knowledge. Rather than strictly following a fixed recipe, they are encouraged to adapt recipes based on dietary needs, ethical consumption, or strategies to reduce food waste. This approach fosters problem-solving skills, creativity, and adaptability, making learning more meaningful and relevant (Skolverket, 2022). Mistakes are viewed as valuable learning opportunities. Students analyse what went wrong from different perspectives, exploring ways to refine their methods and improve outcomes. Constructivism emphasises metacognition, requiring students to reflect on their learning process to develop critical thinking and self-awareness. Discussions and written evaluations help students assess their decision-making, problem-solving, and overall performance. For instance, students in earlier grades and at the E level might simply describe what they did and whether their meal was successful. At C-A levels, they engage in deeper analysis, evaluating why a particular technique was more effective, how ingredient choices influenced nutrition, or how sustainability considerations shaped their meal planning.

Beyond cooking, financial literacy is another key component of Home Economics. Instead of merely presenting numbers, students explain the reasoning behind their financial decisions, such as their selection of food products. Beginners focus on basic budgeting principles, while more advanced students explore long-term financial implications, including cost efficiency, sustainability, and ethical purchasing (Skolverket, 2022). Learning in Home Economics is highly contextualised, meaning knowledge is built in relation to real-life situations. By applying course content to familiar, everyday scenarios, students recognise the relevance of their learning, increasing motivation and engagement. Furthermore, hands-on activities allow students to develop procedural knowledge and internalise concepts through direct experience, making learning more impactful and long lasting.

Group Discussions for Shared Learning

Peer discussions provide students with opportunities to compare strategies, consider different perspectives, and collaboratively construct knowledge. Encouraging open dialogue is essential, as it allows students to challenge each other's ideas, refine their thinking, and deepen their understanding. Reflection plays a key role in this process, ensuring that students not only develop practical skills but also enhance their reasoning and decision-making abilities - both of which are crucial for independent and responsible living. Instead of simply discussing food waste in theory, students engage in complex, hands-on tasks that make learning more tangible. For example, they conduct an audit of their household's food waste, tracking what is discarded and analysing the reasons behind it. Similarly, they compare the environmental impact of locally sourced versus imported foods, gaining insight into how their choices influence sustainability. These activities foster critical thinking and encourage students to make informed, ethical decisions in their daily lives.

A constructivist approach to Home Economics studies ensures that students are active participants in their learning (comp. Skolverket, 2024). By integrating hands-on experiences, reflective practice, and real-world applications, teachers create a dynamic learning environment where students build both practical competence and critical thinking skills. This student-centred model not only enhances academic success but also equips students with essential life skills in health, economics, and sustainability. As a result, they leave school better prepared to navigate real-world challenges, make responsible choices, and understand the direct relevance of their learning to everyday life.

1.5. Minimum Number of Guaranteed Instructional Hours for Home Economics Studies

This section has been included to offer a broader perspective on the subject's framework and didactics, enhancing clarity and comprehension. It is not part of the Swedish edition of the book.

Students in primary school are entitled to a minimum number of guaranteed instructional hours per stage, in this case, middle and upper primary school. This is stated in the Swedish Education Act (2010:800) and the Education Ordinance, *Skolförordningen* (SFS 2011:185). The schedule specifies how these instructional hours should be distributed among the different subjects. The regulation of instructional time is based on the following provisions:

Total instructional time: According to Chapter 10, Section 5 of the Education Act, the total instructional time that students are entitled to during their schooling is regulated.

- **School year and scheduling:**
  Chapters 3, Sections 2-4 and 6 of the Education Ordinance provide guidelines on how the school year should be structured, how schoolwork should be distributed over time, and how students' schedules should be designed.

- **Instructional time and choices:**
  Chapters 9, Sections 3-9 and 11 of the Education Ordinance specify how instructional time should be used, including regulations for language choices, student electives, and school-determined subjects.

- **Regarding the distribution of instructional time,**
  schools have some flexibility within certain limits to adjust how hours are allocated between subjects. The number of hours specified in the schedule for a particular subject or subject group may be reduced by up to 20 percent if the school deems it appropriate based on a specific educational profile. This allows schools some flexibility to tailor instruction according to their pedagogical priorities and students' needs.

As of the autumn term of 2024, the Swedish Parliament has abolished student electives in primary school. The government has decided how the time previously allocated for electives should be redistributed among the other subjects in the schedule. The revised schedule has taken effect for all students in all grades. According to the current schedule, Home Economics has an instructional time of 40 hours per year during lower and middle primary school and 90 hours per year during upper primary school (Skolverket, 2024). This amounts to a total of 130 hours for the entire primary school education. Compared to other subjects, Home Economics has the least instructional time. For example, Physical Education is allocated 600 hours, Mathematics 1,230 hours, while both Music and Art are assigned 240 hours each. This highlights how the subject's allocated time is significantly more limited than many other subjects, despite its importance within the broader educational curriculum.

2. Regulations and Legislation on Teaching in Home Economics Studies

An inspirational image of a traditional HE classroom in a renovated, old school building.
The room is spacious, with high ceilings and sturdy, solid elements.
To reduce echo, wooden materials have been used in the interior design.
By E. Larsson, created using a graphic design program and IKEA's planning tool.

Several regulations and laws govern the work and teaching of Home Economics Studies. This chapter covers the Education Act, the Work Environment Act, and food legislation including the Food Act, the Environmental Code, and local regulations.

This chapter is divided as follows:

2.1. The Education Act and Pedagogy in Home Economics studies
> 2.1.1. Adapted Teaching
> 2.1.2. The Best Interests of the Child
> 2.1.3. Human Rights and Home Economics
> 2.1.4. Teaching about Nutritious Food

2.4.2. Threats, Violence, and Harassment
The Teacher's and Student's Perspectives
"Ongoing Deadly Violence"
Lockdown and Evacuation

The Education Act is the overarching legislation regulating the Swedish school system. It includes provisions regarding the mission of schools, students' rights and obligations, as well as the organisation and responsibilities of schools. Within Home Economics studies, the Education Act governs aspects such as the subject's status and content, as well as requirements for the quality of teaching and assessment. The Work Environment Act aims to ensure a safe and healthy working environment for all employees. In Home Economics studies, this legislation covers issues related to the working environment in kitchen settings, the use of hazardous substances, and ergonomics when handling equipment.

Food legislation consists of various laws and regulations that govern the handling of food to ensure food safety and consumer health. The Food Act plays a key role, outlining provisions on food hygiene, labelling, and food inspection. The Environmental Code is a fundamental law regulating how society should manage and protect the environment. Within Home Economics studies, the Environmental Code is relevant to issues concerning the handling and disposal of chemicals and other environmentally hazardous substances. In addition to national legislation, schools and school authorities may have their own local regulations, such as policies, guidelines, and curricula that govern and guide the work within Home Economics studies at a specific school or municipality.

Several authorities oversee different aspects of the school environment and its regulations. The Swedish Schools Inspectorate (Skolinspektionen) is responsible for evaluating schools from an educational perspective, including aspects of the school environment that affect students' safety and well-being. Although it is not the primary authority for environmental and health protection, it may address noise issues if they influence students' learning conditions. The Swedish National Agency for Education (Skolverket) and the Schools Inspectorate ensure that schools comply with the educational goals and guidelines established by the government and parliament. They monitor and assess schools' operations to maintain high-quality education and regulatory compliance. The Child and Student Representative (Barn- och elevombudet, BEO) operates within the Schools Inspectorate, providing a platform for children and students to report mistreatment and seek support if they feel unfairly treated in school. Together, these authorities collaborate to foster a safe and stimulating learning environment for all students.

The Swedish Work Environment Authority (Arbetsmiljöverket, 2017) supervises the working environment in schools, covering both staff and students. This includes aspects such as noise levels, air quality, ergonomics, and other work environment concerns. The authority has the power to inspect schools and issue injunctions or prohibitions if work environment requirements are not met. The local environmental and health protection board (Miljö- och hälsoskyddsnämnden) is often the primary supervisory authority for school environments concerning environmental and health protection issues. They ensure that schools comply with the Environmental Code and other relevant regulations. Although the Public Health Agency of Sweden (Folkhälsomyndigheten) does not conduct inspections directly, it provides guidelines and recommendations for promoting healthy school environments.

An inadequately designed and inefficient Home Economics classroom can have multiple negative effects on students' learning and well-being (cf. Newsham, 2009). Poor working conditions, such as excessive noise, high temperatures, and inadequate ventilation, can significantly affect both students and teachers, reducing their ability to concentrate and process information effectively, ultimately lowering the quality of instruction (Taylor et al., 2016; Turunen et al., 2014). Moreover, a shortage of kitchen stations limits students' opportunities to actively engage in practical exercises, restricting their ability to develop essential cooking and household skills. This can also result in some students feeling excluded or not receiving adequate attention from the teacher, which contradicts the Education Act's requirement to always prioritise the child's best interests. An optimal learning environment should be accessible to all students.

Another common issue is excessive noise levels. Poor acoustics, insufficient soundproofing, and overly large student groups can significantly disrupt students' concentration and make communication difficult (Arbetsmiljöverket, 2020; cf. Nylander, L., 2020). For students with hearing impairments, this can create an especially stressful and insecure environment. This conflicts with the Education Act's requirement that children's opinions should be considered and that they should have the opportunity to express themselves freely. Noise and poor acoustics can hinder students from actively participating in discussions and influence their overall learning experience.

2.1. The Swedish Education Act and Pedagogy in Home Economics Studies

According to the Swedish Education Act,

---

all students must be guaranteed a learning environment where education is characterised by safety and teaching by a sense of calm and focus.

The Swedish Education Act, Skollagen 5 kap. 3 §.

In practice, this means that a Home Economics classroom must be designed and maintained in a way that promotes a safe and calm learning environment for students, both during theoretical and practical lessons. The classroom should be adapted for teaching and learning, with sufficient space and resources (both material and staff) to ensure that students can work with focus and without disruptions. This may include organising the space to minimise distractions and promote a sense of security and well-being - for example, by having open and appropriately sized workspaces and planning that takes noise levels and air quality into account (Arbetsmiljöverket, 2017; Svenska Institutet för Standarder, 2023).

Teaching in Home Economics must be equitable, ensuring that all students have the same opportunities for learning, regardless of their background or school setting. Gathering for Schools: A National Strategy for Knowledge and Equity *(Samling för skolan – Nationell strategi för kunskap och likvärdighet*, Regeringen, SOU 2017:35) underscores the importance of providing all students with high-quality education. This

Swedish government report outlines a national strategy aimed at improving knowledge levels and promoting educational equity by reducing disparities between schools, strengthening teaching quality, and guaranteeing equal learning opportunities for all students, regardless of their background or place of residence (cf. Scheutz, 2017).

A key factor in achieving effective and equitable education is systematic quality assurance, where all stakeholders within the school system share a common language and understanding of teaching goals and methods (Skolverket, 2019). In practice, this means ensuring consistent access to appropriate facilities, well-maintained equipment, and qualified teachers across schools to prevent inequalities in educational experiences. In practical terms, furniture and equipment should be selected based on their suitability to support teaching and student learning. Beyond the physical environment, it is also essential that the teacher and other staff in the Home Economics classroom create and maintain a positive and inclusive atmosphere where students feel welcome, respected, and acknowledged (considering group size and individual student needs). This contributes to an educational setting where students feel safe and where teaching can be conducted with focus and a sense of calm.

There are two current initiatives that can enhance Home Economics education. A reform in the Education Act (*Skollagen*) (Government Offices of Sweden, Regeringskansliet, 2024) aims to improve students' access to textbooks and other relevant learning materials. This is particularly important for Home Economics, where teaching requires both food supplies and up-to-date resources on nutrition, economics, sustainable consumption, and cooking techniques. Increased access to high quality and current learning materials can contribute to a more equitable education and enhance the overall quality of the subject (cf. Unicef, 2018).

The government (Regeringskansliet, 2023) has initiated an investigation aimed at reducing the administrative burden for preschool and school teachers, which could have a positive impact on Home Economics studies. Home Economics teachers are often responsible for extensive planning, purchasing materials, ensuring safety regulations, and documenting practical activities. Reducing administrative workload would allow teachers to dedicate more time to teaching, student interaction, and developing pedagogical methods.

As part of these efforts, the report *Time for the Teaching Assignment – Measures for Quality Teaching and the Attractiveness of the Teaching Profession* (*Tid för undervisningsuppdraget – åtgärder för god undervisning och läraryrkenas attraktivitet*) (Regeringen, 2025, SOU 2025:26), published on March 3, 2025, proposes several measures to regulate teachers' and preschool teachers' work time through amendments to the Education Act (*Skollagen*). These include a state regulation of the teaching assignment, ensuring that planning and follow-up are explicitly defined as part of teachers' work. Additionally, the report suggests mandatory time allocation for planning and follow-up across all school forms, including after-school centres, as well as limits on teaching hours for compulsory and upper secondary schools. Further recommendations aim to reduce documentation requirements, granting preschools and schools greater flexibility in determining how and when to inform guardians about students' progress. Typically, only one development meeting per school year would be required, with written progress plans focusing solely on academic development. Moreover, the current documentation systems - which are often time-consuming and administratively demanding - are recommended for review to minimise unnecessary workload. Together, these initiatives can improve conditions for both Home Economics teachers and students by reducing workload and ensuring that all learners have access to the necessary resources for high qualitative education.

An inspirational image of a modern HE classroom in an older school building.
By E. Larsson, created using a graphic design program
and IKEA's planning tool.

2.1.1. Adapted Teaching

According to Chapter 1, Section 4, second paragraph of the Swedish Education Act

---

Education must take into account students' different needs. Students should be provided with support and stimulation to

develop as far as possible. The aim should be to compensate for differences in students' ability to benefit from education.

The Swedish Education Act, Skollagen 2010:800

What does this mean in the practical teaching of Home Economics Studies?

This means that teaching must be adapted to meet students' varying needs and abilities in the best possible way. Ideally, individualised teaching should be strived for. The most beneficial approach is for the teacher to work with each student individually to identify their specific needs and tailor the teaching and resources accordingly. This can involve presenting theoretical information through various types of media, offering extra support based on students' abilities and learning styles, and allowing them to demonstrate their knowledge in multiple ways during assessments. In practice, this means that the classroom should be equipped with technology that enables teaching through digital audio-visual tools.

It is also possible to differentiate and thereby adapt tasks for different students. This means that the same learning objectives can be achieved in different ways or that different levels of assignments are offered depending on students' needs and abilities. However, such adaptations require sufficient staff, additional planning time for the teacher, and appropriately timed lessons. Additionally, teachers can provide tailored resources, such as different learning materials, technological aids, or extra guidance and support. In some cases, the Home Economics classroom should include disability-adapted kitchens with height-adjustable work surfaces.

Regarding instruction, clear communication is fundamental. Teachers should be able to communicate expectations, instructions, and learning goals effectively. This may include using various communication methods to ensure that all students understand and can fully participate (e.g., for students with language difficulties or hearing impairments). By considering students' diverse needs and adapting teaching accordingly, educators can create an inclusive and supportive learning environment where all students have the opportunity to develop and reach their full potential.

2.1.2. The Best Interests of the Child

According to Chapter 1, Section 10 of the Education Act, the best interests of the child must always be the guiding principle in all education and activities covered by the Act. The term "child" is defined as any individual under the age of 18, which includes all students participating in Home Economics studies. This means that teaching should be designed with particular attention to children's needs and interests to ensure a safe and stimulating learning environment.

The child's opinion should be clarified as far as possible. Children must have the opportunity to freely express their views on all matters concerning them.

Their opinions should be given weight in relation to their age and maturity. In the preparatory work for the Education Act, it is stated that children's and students' influence extends, for example, to the school cafeteria and, consequently, to meals

The Swedish Education Act, Skollagen 2010:800

For teaching in the Home Economics studies classroom, this means that the child's best interests and their opinions should be central and guiding in lesson planning and execution. As mentioned in the previous section, it is essential to create an inclusive and safe environment where students feel welcome to express their opinions and actively participate in the learning process.

In practice, this involves creating opportunities for open dialogue and discussion, where students' viewpoints and feedback are encouraged and respected. Students should be given the chance, as far as possible, to participate in planning the lessons and making decisions related to, for example, the school cafeteria and meals. This can be achieved by involving them in discussions about which dishes to prepare, how the cafeteria should be organised, and how meals can be improved to better meet their needs and preferences. One way to facilitate this is by establishing a meal committee with student representatives from different grade levels. The teaching should also be adapted to students' age, maturity, and individual needs. This means offering a variety of activities and tasks that are appropriate and engaging for each student.

The best interests of the child and equitable education also mean that students who require special adaptations receive the support and pedagogical adjustments they are entitled to. Students who are restless or struggle to follow hygiene and safety regulations in the Home Economics classroom should be provided with appropriate forms of support. This also includes the teacher's duty of supervision. This responsibility is based on existing regulatory frameworks. The duty of supervision means that the legal guardian of a child is responsible for ensuring that the child's needs are met and that the child is not exposed to harm (*Parental Code, Föräldrabalken*, SFS 1949:381, Chapter 6, Section 2). When a child is at school, this responsibility is transferred from the guardian to the school authority. The school authority holds the ultimate responsibility for creating a safe and secure environment, ensuring that the child's needs are met, that they are protected from harm, and that they do not pose a risk to others.

In terms of physical space, prioritising the child's best interest means designing the Home Economics studies classroom to be accessible and inclusive for all students, regardless of disabilities or special needs. This includes ensuring enough space for movement and different activities while fostering a safe and stimulating learning environment. From a material perspective, this means that the classroom should be equipped with appropriate tools, ingredients, and resources, allowing students to explore different aspects of the subject in a hands-on and varied manner. Students should also have opportunities to participate in selecting tools, ingredients, and kitchen equipment used in the lessons.

However, disparities in available materials and equipment between schools or classes may create unequal learning conditions, which contradicts the Education Act's requirement for equitable education (cf. Bergström, 2013). A more concerning scenario arises when the condition of the Home Economics studies classroom is severely deteriorated, making practical lessons a continuous safety hazard for students. This could include poorly functioning ventilation systems that increase the risk of fire or health issues, or unsafe tools and equipment that pose injury risks. A lack of safety measures directly conflicts with the Education Act's principle that the child's best interests should be the foundation of Home Economics studies, ensuring that student health and safety are prioritised.

2.1.3. Human Rights and Home Economics

Education shall be designed in accordance with fundamental democratic values and human rights, including the inviolability of human life, individual freedom and integrity, the equal value of all people, gender equality, and solidarity among individuals.

Everyone involved in education must promote human rights and actively counteract all forms of degrading treatment.

The Swedish Education Act, Skollagen (2010:800)

The provisions in Chapter 1, Section 5, influence all teaching within the Swedish school system. These principles are highlighted in the new national curriculum for compulsory schooling, Lgr22, which incorporates fundamental democratic values and human rights.

The school shall actively work to promote gender equality. This includes embodying and conveying equal rights, opportunities, and responsibilities for girls and boys, women and men. In accordance with fundamental values, the school shall also encourage interaction among students regardless of gender identity. Through education, students should develop an understanding of how different perceptions of femininity and masculinity can influence individuals' opportunities. The school should thus contribute to students' ability to critically examine gender patterns and how they may limit people's life choices and conditions.

Through an environmental perspective, students gain opportunities both to take responsibility for the environment they can directly influence and to develop a personal approach to overarching and global environmental issues. Teaching should highlight how societal functions and our ways of living and working can be adapted to promote sustainable development.

Swedish National Agency for Education,
(Skolverket) 2022, Lgr22

These principles have been partially integrated into the core content of the Home Economics curriculum. A well-planned approach to teaching the subject contributes to the promotion of fundamental democratic values and human rights in accordance with the Swedish Education Act. The subject's objectives and core content provide a comprehensive pedagogical foundation for students to develop the knowledge, skills, and attitudes necessary for active participation in society and for contributing to a more just and sustainable world.

Within the curriculum's focus on lifestyle habits, two key areas are highlighted: the division of household labour from a gender equality perspective and resource management. These areas encompass decision-making regarding the selection and use of food and other goods, as well as the impact of production, transportation, and recycling on human health, the economy, and the environment.

1. Division of Household Labour from a Gender Equality Perspective

By discussing and analysing household labour distribution from a gender equality perspective, Home Economics studies encourages students to reflect on and challenge traditional gender roles and norms. This fosters respect for individual freedom and integrity, as well as the equal value of all individuals. By promoting critical thinking on issues of gender equality and equity, educators can actively counteract all forms of discrimination and support the development of a fairer and more inclusive societal structure.

2. **Resources management**

Teaching about resource management emphasises the importance of taking responsibility for one's actions and their impact on human health, the economy, and the environment. By guiding students to make informed and sustainable choices regarding the selection and use of food and other goods, the subject reinforces core democratic values such as solidarity and consideration for the well-being of others and the environment. It also helps students develop an awareness of human rights, including the right to a healthy environment and sustainable development.

Home Economics studies can serve as a platform for fostering awareness and understanding of human rights. By integrating topics such as respect for individual freedom and integrity, the equal value of all people and gender equality into classroom activities, students can learn to understand and respect diverse rights and values. Additionally, teaching in this subject can be used as a tool to actively counter all forms of degrading treatment. Practical assignments and group work create opportunities for discussions on cooperation, respect, tolerance, and solidarity. A significant responsibility falls on the teacher and their subject expertise. It is crucial that the teacher establishes a safe and inclusive environment where students feel respected and accepted regardless of their background, culture, gender, or other factors.

It is essential that students are given sufficient time and space to meaningfully understand and apply these concepts. A significant number of teachers surveyed have expressed concern about the scheduling of the subject and the reduction of instructional hours, as well as the challenge of large student groups. These factors can create several issues regarding the teaching of labour division and resource management. A reduction in instructional hours and large class sizes can make it difficult to provide students with adequate time to discuss and reflect on key topics and concepts. This, in turn, limits their ability to develop a deep understanding of the subject and apply it to their own lives. When instructional hours are reduced, teachers often prioritise the most essential parts of the curriculum, which frequently results in topics such as gender equality in labour division, resource management, and personal finance being overlooked (Swedish Schools Inspectorate, Skolinspektionen, 2018).

A decrease in instructional time and large class sizes also hinder the practical application of knowledge. Since topics such as labour division and resource management require hands-on learning experiences for students to fully grasp them, limited time and large groups reduce opportunities for practical exercises. This further restricts individualised feedback and support. In large groups, it becomes challenging for teachers to provide each student with the necessary feedback and guidance to develop and refine their skills. Consequently, some students may fall behind or fail to reach their full potential. Additionally, large class sizes make it difficult to tailor instruction to individual students' needs and circumstances, potentially leaving some students feeling overlooked or without the support they need to succeed.

An inspirational image of "*Teaching about Nutritious Food*".
By E. Larsson/Artelinas.

2.1.4. Teaching about Nutritious Food

The Swedish Education Act mandates that meals provided in compulsory school forms must be both free of charge and nutritionally adequate (Education Act 2010:800; Chapter 10, Section 10 for Compulsory

School, Chapter 11, Section 13 for Special Schools, Chapter 12, Section 10 for Schools for Students with Disabilities, and Chapter 13, Section 10 for Sami Schools). This legal requirement applies to both public and independent schools.

The Swedish Schools Inspectorate is responsible for ensuring compliance with these legal provisions. Their role includes conducting inspections and evaluations of schools to verify that they meet the standards set for school meals. This may involve reviewing meal routines, menus, and meal quality to ensure that students have access to healthy and nutritious options at no additional cost. If a school fails to meet these requirements, the Schools Inspectorate can issue recommendations or corrective measures to address deficiencies and ensure that students' needs are met. In this way, the Schools Inspectorate serves as a regulatory authority to guarantee that schools fulfil their obligations concerning school meals.

The requirement that school meals must be both free and nutritionally balanced is directly linked to the teaching of Home Economics. This means that instruction should not only enhance students' understanding of healthy cooking and nutrition but also ensure that meal preparation in practice is cost-free and that the meals prepared meet nutritional standards.

The Swedish Education Act does not provide a precise definition of the term nutritionally adequate. However, the government has stressed that Swedish nutritional recommendations should serve as a basis for determining what constitutes a nutritionally balanced meal. Furthermore, it is considered part of the curriculum's intentions that students should have access to varied and nutritious food and eat lunch together with other students and adults.

> *"... It can be considered part of the curriculum's intentions that students have access to varied and nutritious food and eat lunch together with other students and adults."*
>
> *The Swedish Government, 2009, Prop. 2009/10:165, 374*

National Guidelines for School Meals

The Swedish Food Agency (Livsmedelsverket, 2021a) has issued national guidelines for school meals to promote healthy eating habits and ensure nutritionally adequate meals for students. These guidelines serve as a framework for schools and other stakeholders within the school meal system to guarantee that students are offered nutritious and balanced meals that contribute to their health and well-being. By providing clear guidance, the Swedish Food Agency helps ensure a consistent and high standard of school meals across the country. These guidelines are based on current research and expertise in nutrition and healthy eating. They are designed to support students' health, concentration, and learning. By adhering to these national recommendations, schools can ensure that their meals are nutritionally balanced and align with dietary guidelines for a healthy lifestyle. This ensures that students receive the necessary nutrients for optimal growth and development, thereby enhancing their ability to learn and perform academically.

Home Economics plays a crucial role in increasing young people's knowledge of healthy living. According to the Swedish Food Agency's *Riksmaten Ungdom* survey (2018), approximately 21% of young people in Sweden are overweight, and 4% suffer from obesity. Educational background significantly influences healthy habits, as overweight and obesity are more common among children whose parents have a lower level of education and in sparsely populated areas (cf. Persson, 2016). A smaller study included youth who were not attending upper secondary school (gymnasium), revealing that 42% of them were overweight, with 23% classified as obese. Additionally, nearly half of these participants reported not feeling well. The *Riksmaten Ungdom* survey included over 3,000 students from grade 5, grade 8, and year 2 of upper secondary school. In the separate study on non-upper secondary school students, 81 young people from across Sweden participated.

According to the Swedish Food Agency's meal model, which is intended for planning and evaluating public meal services, food should be safe, tasty, nutritious, integrated, sustainable, and enjoyable (Livsmedelsverket, 2023a; cf. Gustafsson et al., 2006). Although the meal model is designed for public meals in healthcare, schools, and elderly care, its principles can be adapted and applied to meals in Home Economics lessons. This involves considering the specific conditions of the subject and structuring lessons around the six key components of the meal model to ensure that students gain a holistic understanding of what is required to create good and sustainable meals. The meal model addresses the core content of the subject, and by focusing on aspects such as taste, nutritional content, food safety, environmental impact, and the integration of meals into daily life, students can develop their knowledge and skills in Home Economics.

Teaching should therefore integrate a holistic view of meals, where students learn to see a meal as more than just the food that is prepared and eaten together. It is also about creating a pleasant atmosphere around the meal and using available resources in a thoughtful way. Even if this is not always directly applied in Home Economics lessons, knowledge of the Meal Model can be valuable for students in areas such as personal finance and consumer education. For example, this knowledge can be useful when planning meals in the future or making budgets and price comparisons, as it provides insight into important criteria to consider when choosing food, ingredients, services, as well as suppliers and meal planning.

The Swedish Food Agency provides a wealth of material on food, meals, and health, which can help schools and teachers in Home Economics studies to follow recommendations:

- **Balanced Meals (Food or Dietary Circle)**
  School meals should be balanced and include a variety of foods from different food groups, including fruits, vegetables, grains, protein-rich foods, and dairy products.

- **Meal Proportions (The Plate Model)**
  The plate model is an educational tool that illustrates how to distribute food on the plate to increase the proportion of vegetables and create a well-balanced meal.

- **Nutrient-Rich Beverages**
  Recommendations include guidelines on which beverages should be offered with school meals, such as water, milk, or other low-sugar drinks.

- **Reducing Salt, Sugar, and Fat**
  The guidelines provide recommendations for reducing the amount of salt, sugar, and saturated fat in school meals to promote healthy eating habits.

- **Allergies, Sensitivities, and Special Diets**
  Meals should be inclusive for all students. Food allergies are common in childhood, with milk protein and egg allergies being the most prevalent. Recommendations and guidelines include information on alternative products with high nutritional value.

An inspirational image of cooking in a HE classroom.
By E. Larsson/Artelinas.

Support for Home Economics Teachers

The Swedish Food Agency bases its dietary recommendations on the latest research, a collection of scientific studies, and proven experience. For a teacher, it can be challenging to navigate food trends, new research findings, and media messages about what is considered healthy to eat.

The Swedish Food Agency provides extensive support for Home Economics studies by offering knowledge, resources, and tools to promote healthy eating habits and cooking skills among students. Their recommendations and guidelines serve as a key foundation for teaching the subject. They aim to enhance students' understanding of healthy eating and cooking, food safety, and educate them on making informed and nutritious food choices.

- **Nutritional Information:**
  The Swedish Food Agency provides information on the nutritional content of various foods, and how to create balanced and nutritious meals. It includes facts about nutrients, food additives, bacteria, dietary supplements, as well as unwanted substances and environmental toxins.
  - The Nordic Nutrition Recommendations (NNR 2023):
    The latest and most comprehensive compilation of research on food and health. The NNR describes dietary habits that promote good health both in the short and long term and provides recommendations on energy and nutrient intake.
    For the first time, NNR 2023 also considers the environmental and climate impact of our food choices. These recommendations will serve as the foundation for future dietary guidelines in Sweden and other Nordic countries.

  - The Food Database:
    The Food Database contains information on more than 2,400 foods and dishes. Each food item in the database includes detailed values for over 50 nutrients and components.

  - Facts About Energy and Energy Needs:
    There is information available on basic human energy requirements, including the energy used at rest, the thermogenic effect of food, and physical activity levels. The Food Database provides energy content data for over 2,000 different foods, calculated using standard factors for protein, carbohydrates, fats, alcohol, and

dietary fibres. Carbohydrates also include sugar alcohols and organic acids.

- **Food Hygiene and Handling:**
  Through its resources and publications, the Swedish Food Agency provides tips and advice on food hygiene, food handling, and safe cooking - covering what happens to food during preparation and how packaging materials such as plastic, paper, glass, and metal can affect food.

- **Dietary Advice and Recommendations:**
  The Swedish Food Agency provides advice and recommendations for a healthy and balanced diet, including how to incorporate different food groups into daily meals.
  - The Keyhole Label:
    A label that indicates a food product is a healthier choice within its category. To use the Keyhole label, a product must meet specific criteria, including less sugar and salt, increased amount of whole grains and fibres, and healthier fats.

  - The Plate Model (found on the homepage)

The Plate Model by The Swedish Food Agency homepage

The Plate model is an educational tool that illustrates how to distribute food on a plate to increase the proportion of vegetables and create a balanced meal. According to the plate model, about one-fifth of the meal should consist of protein sources such as meat, fish, eggs, or legumes. The proportion of vegetables and carbohydrates (such as potatoes, pasta, bread, or grains) is more flexible and can be adjusted based on an individual's level of physical activity. Those who are more active require larger amounts of energy-rich carbohydrates, while those with a sedentary lifestyle may reduce them.

- o <u>The New Food Circle</u>

The New Food Circle by The Swedish Food Agency homepage

To promote more sustainable eating habits, the Swedish Food Agency has developed a greener version of the Food Circle, where plant-based alternatives play a significantly larger role than before. Today, there is a wide range of plant-based foods, which is reflected in the updated Food Circle. For example, the dairy section has been expanded to include plant-based alternatives such as "gurts" and vegan drinks.

- o Diet Check (Matvanekollen):
  A simple quick test that also provides tips on how to eat healthier.

- **Environmental Awareness:**
  The Swedish Food Agency provides tips on how to make cooking more environmentally friendly and reduce the environmental impact of food. This includes reducing meat portions and eating more vegetarian meals, choosing sustainably caught or farmed fish, opting for long-lasting fruits and vegetables, and minimising food waste by storing food properly, planning purchases, and making use of leftovers.

- **Healthy Meal Ideas:**
  The Swedish Food Agency offers meal ideas that are nutritious and balanced, such as Keyhole-labelled and low-sodium dishes, as well as themed recipes, including chicken recipes, vegetarian dishes, and meat-based meals.

- **Educational Materials:**
  The Swedish Food Agency produces educational materials and resources tailored for use in Home Economics education:
  - o *"Svinnrik"*
    A teaching resource for Home Economics teachers aimed at educating students on how to save money and protect the environment by making better use of food.

o "Food for All Senses" – Sensory Training Using the Sapere Method
   A teaching guide for grades 4–6 on sensory training, focusing on experiencing and exploring the environment through our senses - sight, hearing, smell, taste, and touch.

o "The School Meal"
   The Swedish Food Agency has created an inspirational guide for school leaders and educators called The School Meal - An Important Part of a Good School. This material can be used in various subjects and serves as an excellent starting point for meaningful discussions.

Systematic Quality Work on Food and Meals in Schools

The preparatory works of the Swedish Education Act highlight school meals as an integrated part of education (prop. 2009/10:165, 872). This means that the regulations on systematic quality work (Chapter 4, Section 3 of the Education Act, *Skollagen*) also apply to ensuring nutritious school meals. Each school authority is therefore obligated to continuously plan, follow up, and improve education, which includes documenting systematic quality work (Chapter 4, Section 6). To ensure the quality of school meals, nutritional assessments, such as nutrient calculations, should be a central part of meal planning, implementation, and follow-up. Additionally, it is important for schools to include descriptions of their work with school meals as part of their quality efforts. This is especially relevant for Home Economics studies, where knowledge of nutrition and meal planning is essential.

According to the Swedish National Agency for Education (Livsmedelsverket, 2010; 2021), school meals play a significant role as an integrated educational tool in schools' work on lifestyle, environment, and health. They are also an important part of the school's social development efforts, as they create opportunities for discussions on values and norms and help identify students in need of extra support. The goal of an educationally focused meal is to promote interaction between adults and children, fostering a positive attitude toward meals and a natural relationship with food. By integrating meals into the educational process, schools can create an environment that supports both social interaction and learning about healthy eating habits. Adults play a key role as positive role models, and by enjoying tasty meals together in a pleasant atmosphere, both students and staff can contribute to a positive dining experience, facilitating social interaction and recovery.

According to the Lgr22 curriculum, it is clear that the globalisation of modern society requires individuals to navigate and appreciate cultural diversity, and schools serve as a central platform for strengthening this ability. By using meals as an opportunity to explore and appreciate different food cultures and traditions, schools can foster curiosity and understanding of diversity. Additionally, school meals play a significant role in promoting health, sustainability, and social development. By providing a shared platform for students to engage in meaningful conversations about values and inclusion, meals contribute to creating an environment where all students feel seen and included.

The education shall be based on scientific principles and proven experience.

Meals in the Home Economics Classroom

The preparatory work for the Swedish Education Act (prop. 2009/10:165) emphasises that school meals are an integrated part of education and should be treated as such. In Home Economics studies, this can have at least three implications: theoretical learning, practical cooking, and systematic quality work. Theoretical learning allows students to gain knowledge about nutrition, healthy eating habits, and how to plan and prepare nutritious meals. By understanding nutritional needs and how different foods affect health, students can develop a deeper appreciation of a balanced diet, promoting their well-being.

Practical cooking gives students the opportunity to apply their nutritional knowledge in real-life scenarios by planning and preparing meals that meet nutritional standards. This includes selecting nutrient-rich ingredients and cooking them in a healthy way. Quality work involves integrating systematic quality assessments into meal-related education. Students learn the importance of evaluating the nutritional content and quality of food. They can use nutritional calculations and other assessment methods to plan and ensure that the meals they prepare are nutritious and balanced.

Meals in the Home Economics classroom can be considered educational for several reasons. Experiential learning takes place through hands-on activities, where students gain experience by planning, preparing, and cooking meals. Skill reinforcement occurs through repetitive practical exercises, helping students develop skills in nutrition, cooking techniques, and food safety, applying knowledge in real-life situations. Responsibility and independence are fostered as students participate in planning, cooking, and serving meals, practicing skills such as responsibility, teamwork, and independence. They may also make decisions about recipe selection, ingredient purchases, and meal planning under teacher guidance.

Meal preparation in Home Economics studies is integrated into lesson and course planning, aligning with the subject's purpose, core content, and knowledge criteria. The learning process incorporates multiple educational development areas. Students learn different methods of meal preparation, gaining an understanding of healthy meals and nutrition by working with various ingredients and recipes. They develop an understanding of nutritional content in different foods and how to create balanced and nutritious meals. By experimenting with ingredients, they explore flavours and textures, fostering an interest in diverse and nutritious food choices.

Meals in Home Economics also offer social and cultural learning opportunities. Social interaction is encouraged as preparing and sharing meals with classmates strengthens cooperation and a sense of community in the classroom. Exploring recipes from different food traditions, allowing students to gain insights into various cultures and eating habits, develop cultural awareness. Finally, education in Home Economics studies is based on scientific research and proven experience, ensuring that students receive relevant, high-quality knowledge and skills for life.

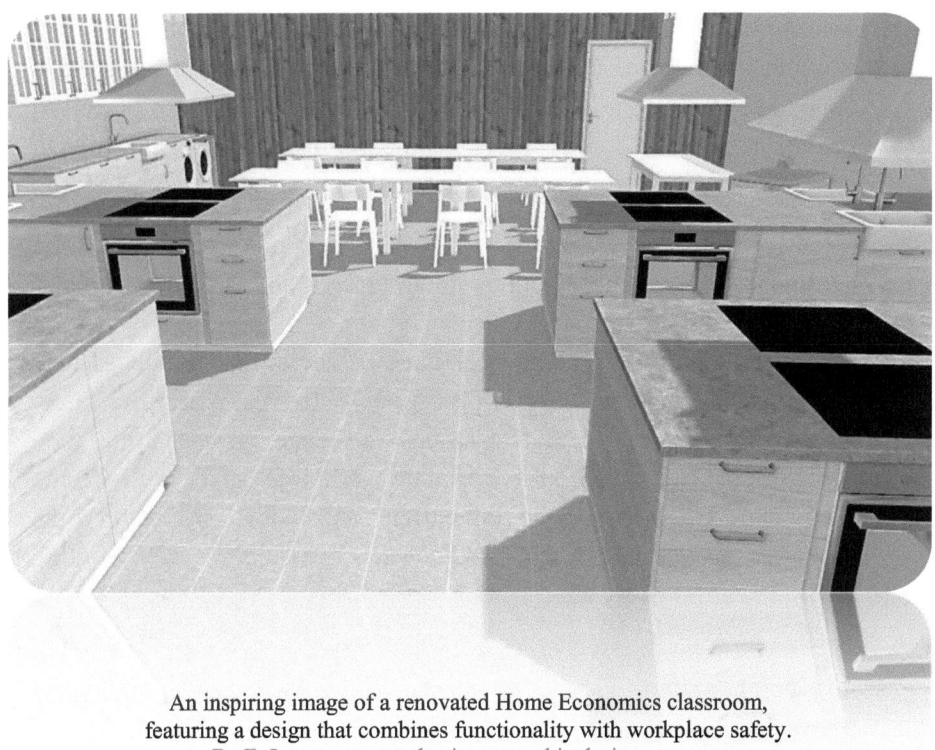

An inspiring image of a renovated Home Economics classroom,
featuring a design that combines functionality with workplace safety.
By E. Larsson, created using a graphic design program
and IKEA's planning tool.

2.2. Workplace Safety, the Work Environment Act, and the Home Economics Classroom

2.2.1. Workplace Safety

The Swedish Education Act (2010:800) also covers aspects of workplace safety: all students must receive high-quality instruction under safe conditions and work in a secure learning environment. Physical safety includes several aspects (Anttalainen, Manninen et al., 2014), such as mechanical and physical hazards, risks of accidents, chemical and biological exposures, as well as physical strain and ergonomics. Since

Sweden has moved away from strict regulations regarding facilities and equipment for Home Economics education, which were in place when compulsory schooling was introduced, there is not always a perceived need to inspect the spaces where instruction takes place. This leads to increased risks concerning workplace safety.

Workplace safety is of the utmost importance in all work environments to protect employees from accidents and injuries. This also includes the school and the Home Economics classroom, where students and teachers collaborate in cooking and other educational activities. Workplace safety also means complying with legislation and regulations concerning food and hygiene. It is important to examine workplace safety in the Home Economics classroom based on current legislation and identify the measures that need to be considered to ensure a safe working environment for everyone.

The Public Health Agency of Sweden states in a regulation, Article 22056, Supervisory Guidance on Health Protection in Schools and Preschools, the following:

Schools and preschools are covered by the Environmental Code, whose overarching purpose is to protect human health and the environment from potential hazards. The Environmental and Health Protection Committee must pay special attention to schools and preschools in its supervision, according to Section 45 of the Ordinance (1998:899) on environmentally hazardous activities.

Public Health Agency of Sweden, (Folkhälsomyndigheten), 2022 a.

In practice, this means that schools and preschools are subject to laws and regulations governing environmental and health protection. The Environmental Code (1998:808) is a central piece of legislation that contains fundamental provisions, supplemented by ordinances and agency regulations that specify these provisions. The Environmental Code aims to protect human health and the environment from harm and nuisances.

According to this law, the Environmental and Health Protection Committee (Miljö- och hälsoskyddsnämnden), which is part of the municipal administration, must pay special attention to schools and preschools in its supervision. This means that the committee is responsible for ensuring that schools and preschools comply with legal requirements and maintain a safe and healthy environment for both staff and children. Schools and preschools are also required to notify the municipal Environmental and Health Protection Committee (miljö- och hälsoskyddsnämnden) before commencing their operations. In summary, strict laws and regulations govern environmental and health protection in schools and preschools, and municipal authorities have supervisory responsibilities to ensure compliance with these regulations.

The person responsible for a school or preschool must conduct ongoing, systematic work to prevent the premises or activities from negatively affecting human health or the environment. This is done through self-monitoring.

Public Health Agency of Sweden, (Folkhälsomyndigheten), 2022 b.

In practice, this means that the person responsible for a school or preschool must actively work to ensure that the premises and activities do not negatively influence human health or the environment. This requires continuous and systematic efforts to identify and manage potential risks and hazards that may arise in the Home Economics classroom. By implementing self-monitoring, the school commits to overseeing and evaluating various aspects of its operations, such as hygiene, safety, and environmental impact. This involves regularly inspecting the premises, assessing routines and procedures, and taking measures to prevent problems and reduce risks. The purpose of self-monitoring is to ensure compliance with all legal requirements and guidelines while maintaining a safe and healthy environment for both staff and students. It serves as a crucial tool for promoting a secure and healthy school environment and preventing potential accidents or health issues.

2.2.2. The Work Environment Act and Its Application in the Home Economics Classroom

In Sweden, The Work Environment Act (Arbetsmiljölagen, AML, 1977:1160) establishes regulations and guidelines to ensure a safe and healthy working environment. The AML also applies to educational institutions, including schools and Home Economics classrooms. This legislation requires schools to comply with the law and implement appropriate measures to prevent accidents and protect both students and staff from hazards.

Within the framework of the Work Environment Act, several aspects are particularly relevant to the work conducted in the Home Economics classroom:

1. **Work Environment Policy:**
   According to the AML, the employer - which in this context may be the school or educational institution - must establish a work environment policy that clearly defines the employer's responsibility for workplace safety and outlines the measures required to maintain a safe and healthy environment (Swedish Work Environment Authority, Arbetsmiljöverket, 2023a).

2. **Systematic Work Environment Management:**
   The employer is obligated to implement systematic work environment management to prevent illness and accidents. This involves continuously identifying, assessing, and addressing risks in the workplace, including those present in the Home Economics classroom. Work environment issues can be addressed at multiple levels: schools often have union representatives, such as those from The Swedish Teachers' Union, (Sveriges Lärare), as well as a safety representative who

can raise concerns with the safety committee, which consists of representatives from both the unions and the employer (Swedish Work Environment Authority, Arbetsmiljöverket, 2024a).

According to the AML, students have the right to appoint student safety representatives who can participate in the school's work environment efforts. In workplaces with multiple safety representatives, it is common for one to be designated as the chief safety representative. The chief safety representative is responsible for coordinating the work of the safety representatives and serves as their external representative. Their responsibilities extend across the entire workplace and include handling issues with the employer that affect multiple safety areas.

Trade unions often appoint regional safety representatives to represent employees at workplaces where no local safety representatives are present (Swedish Work Environment Authority, Arbetsmiljöverket, 2024a). These regional safety representatives have the same responsibilities and rights as local safety representatives and can represent employees regardless of their union affiliation. In practice, it is uncommon for a regional safety representative to be non-unionised, although it is theoretically possible. Additionally, regional safety representatives have the right to act in workplaces where local safety representatives exist, provided there is at least one union member from the organisation the representative belongs to. However, regional safety representatives cannot represent employees at workplaces with an established safety committee.

In certain situations, collaboration between local and regional safety representatives can be beneficial, particularly in advocating for workplace safety improvements. Regional safety representatives can offer an external and objective perspective, which may strengthen efforts to implement workplace safety enhancements.

3. **The Workplace Design**
   The Work Environment Act requires that workplaces be designed in a manner that ensures safety and health for those working there. This includes the layout of the Home Economics classroom, covering aspects such as planning, equipment, noise levels, and ventilation (Swedish Work Environment Authority, Arbetsmiljöverket, 2017; 2024b; Boverket, 2024).

4. **Protective Equipment**
   According to the AML, employers must provide necessary protective equipment to minimise the risk of workplace injuries. In the Home Economics classroom, this includes protective clothing such as aprons, protective gloves when needed, and other safety measures when handling hazardous substances such as detergents and cleaning agents. Additionally, hygiene precautions must be taken to prevent the spread of illness (e.g., COVID-19, Salmonella).

5. **Training and Information:**
   The employer is responsible for ensuring that both staff and students receive adequate training and information regarding workplace safety and safe practices in the Home Economics classroom. This may include training in the use of kitchen equipment, food handling, fire and accident prevention measures, and first aid.

Safety Regulations for Work in the Home Economics Classroom

Safety regulations are essential for ensuring a secure working environment for students in Home Economics studies. By following these rules, the risk of accidents and injuries can be minimised, especially when using machines or handling sharp objects. Both staff and students must be aware of potential risks and understand how to maintain proper workplace safety in the Home Economics classroom.

It is crucial that teachers and staff establish and consistently follow clear safety practices to protect everyone in the Home Economics classroom. This fosters a strong safety culture and helps prevent accidents by promoting clarity, compliance, and continuous improvement. Examples of workplace safety-enhancing practices include:

- o Inform students about the classroom rules, both in written and oral form.
- o Inform students about hygiene regulations.
- o Inform students about workplace risks and protective equipment.
- o Inspect the classroom's machines and appliances.
- o Conduct and document risk assessments continuously based on a checklist.
- o Ensure that first aid equipment is available.
- o Inform substitute teachers about relevant documents and procedures

By following a predetermined routine, teachers and staff ensure the safety and well-being of both students and personnel in the Home Economics classroom. This is essential for preventing accidents and injuries. Providing clear information about risks, safety measures, and necessary equipment ensures that everyone has equal and sufficient knowledge of the factors affecting safety in an environment where machines and tools are regularly used.

When safety practices are consistently followed, a culture of safety and awareness is fostered among students and staff. This helps reduce the risk of accidents by ensuring that everyone understands and respects established safety procedures while maintaining a standard of compliance expected from all participants. By documenting and continuously monitoring these practices, any deficiencies or areas for improvement can be identified, allowing corrective actions to be taken and enhancing safety measures over time.

Clear rules play a fundamental role in students' educational experience by establishing a structured working environment where expectations and acceptable behaviours are clearly defined. At the same time, safety regulations support students in developing responsibility and discipline (cf. Belt, 2013). Several safety rules apply to student activities in Home Economics studies, which may include the following:

- Never run in the classroom.
- Never throw objects in the classroom.
- No playing during the work process.
- Always return tools and materials to their designated places.
- Do not use machines without receiving proper instructions.
- Wipe the floor if you spill.
- Follow hygiene regulations in kitchen work and leave all surfaces dry and spotless after use.

By following these safety rules, students learn to take responsibility for their own and others' safety, as well as the importance of following instructions and regulations - skills that are essential both in school and the workplace. Rules on cleaning up and maintaining tidy work areas promote good hygiene and contribute to a pleasant, organised working environment.

The Physical Work Environment of the Home Economics Classroom
(Part of the Material Framework Conditions for the Subject)

There are several framework conditions covered by the Work Environment Act regarding the physical environment of the Home Economics studies classroom. These aspects will be addressed in more detail later in the trilogy's second book, in *The Materiel Framework Factors in Home Economics Education*, which discusses the material framework conditions. However, here is an overview:

1. **Sufficient space and good lighting**
   to ensure that work can be carried out safely and efficiently:
   - In Sweden, classroom design, including Home Economics classrooms, must comply with the Work Environment Act and the Swedish National Board of Housing, Building, and Planning's Building Regulations (BBR), which set standards for space allocation, lighting, and general safety.
   - According to the Swedish Work Environment Authority (Arbetsmiljöverket), sufficient space is essential to minimise the risk of injuries, ensure safe movement, and facilitate practical work such as cooking. Proper lighting is also crucial to avoid eyestrain and ensure safety when handling kitchen equipment.

2. **Optimal accessibility**
   is crucial so that all students, including those with disabilities, can work without obstacles or risks of accidents:
   - The Discrimination Act (Diskrimineringslagen, 2008:567) and the Planning and Building Act (Plan- och bygglagen, 2010:900) mandate that school facilities must be accessible to all students, including those with

disabilities. This includes adjustments such as ramps, height-adjustable workstations, adapted kitchen tools, and visual or auditory aids for students with sensory impairments. The Swedish Agency for Participation (Myndigheten för delaktighet, MFD) provides guidelines on how educational spaces should be designed to support equal participation for all students.

3. **Good ventilation and noise adjustments**
   to maintain a healthy work environment:
   - The Work Environment Act requires schools to provide a safe and healthy indoor climate. The Swedish Work Environment Authority's provisions on the indoor environment (AFS 2009:2) highlight the importance of proper ventilation to prevent air contamination from cooking fumes, dust, and allergens. Poor ventilation can lead to headaches, fatigue, and respiratory issues, particularly when working with gas stoves or strong-smelling ingredients.
   - Noise levels in Home Economics classrooms should also be controlled, as excessive background noise from kitchen appliances, students, and ventilation systems can increase stress and make it harder to follow instructions.

4. **Optimal hygienic conditions**
   to ensure that cooking and other activities can be conducted safely and hygienically:
   - In Sweden, the Food Act (Livsmedelslagen, 2006:804) and regulations from the National Food Agency (Livsmedelsverket) establish hygiene standards that must be followed in food preparation environments, including school kitchens. These regulations require that there are adequate washing stations, separate areas for

raw and cooked food handling, and clear routines for cleaning surfaces and equipment.

- Schools must also follow hygiene guidelines concerning illnesses - students and staff who exhibit symptoms of foodborne illnesses, such as norovirus, should not participate in food preparation.

5. **Good ergonomic conditions,**
meaning that furniture and equipment in the Home Economics classroom should be ergonomically designed to minimise the risk of physical strain and health issues, such as back problems and muscle injuries.

- According to the Swedish Work Environment Authority's provisions on ergonomics (Arbetsmiljöverkets författningssamling, AFS 2012:2), schools must ensure that students and staff can work in positions that do not cause strain or injury. This means that countertops, sinks, and stoves should be at appropriate heights for different users.
- Heavy kitchen tools and ingredients should be stored in easily accessible locations to avoid unnecessary lifting. Prolonged standing should also be minimised by providing ergonomic mats or seating options when possible.

6. **Up-to-date and functional safety measures**
to ensure that the Home Economics classroom is equipped with appropriate safety devices and fire extinguishing equipment in accordance with current safety regulations, reducing the risk of accidents and injuries.

- The Swedish Civil Contingencies Agency (Myndigheten för samhällsskydd och beredskap, MSB) and the Swedish Work Environment Authority set fire safety and emergency preparedness regulations. Schools are required to have functioning fire extinguishers, fire blankets, first-aid kits, and clearly marked emergency exits.

- Teachers and students must be trained in handling kitchen fires, such as grease fires, which require fire blankets or CO_2 extinguishers rather than water (Brandsskydsföreningen, 2023)
- The presence of gas stoves or electrical kitchen equipment also necessitates regular maintenance and safety checks.

This expanded version integrates the relevant Swedish laws, agencies, and regulations while providing a clearer picture of their role in ensuring safety and accessibility in Home Economics classrooms.

An inspiring image of a renovated HE classroom in an older school building,
featuring a design that combines high hygiene standards
with an optimally structured pedagogical space.
By E. Larsson, created using a graphic design program
and IKEA's planning tool.

2.3. Food Legislation and the Home Economics Classroom

In Sweden, kitchen and food handling are regulated by several national hygiene regulations and provisions issued by the National Food Agency (Livsmedelsverket). Sweden also adheres to EU legislation on food handling and hygiene. In addition to these regulations, there are specific rules and guidelines (e.g., the Education Act, Skollagen) that apply specifically to teaching in Home Economics.

1. **The Food Act (Livsmedelslag, 2006:804)**
   This is the overarching law regulating food handling in Sweden. It establishes the requirements for safe food management and is responsible for protecting consumer health.

2. **Regulations Issued by the National Food Agency (Statens livsmedelsverks författningssamling, SLVFS)**
   The National Food Agency has issued multiple regulations covering different aspects of food handling. Examples include *"Hygiene Regulations for Food Establishments"* (SLVFS 2001:30) and *"Food Hygiene, HACCP, and Internal Controls"* (SLVFS 2006:27). These regulations outline detailed requirements and guidelines for food hygiene and safety.

3. **EU Regulations:**
   Sweden also complies with EU legislation on food handling and hygiene. Notable examples include Regulation (EC) No. 852/2004 and Regulation (EC) No. 853/2004 on food hygiene, which set out basic hygiene requirements for food businesses. Additionally, the European Commission's guidance on Regulation (EC) No. 852/2004 provides further clarification on compliance.

4. **Hazard Analysis and Critical Control Points (HACCP)**
   HACCP is a system designed to identify and control risks in food handling. Food businesses are required to develop and implement HACCP programs to ensure food safety. Given its numerous benefits, HACCP can also be applied in Home Economics classrooms, serving both as an educational tool and as a means to maintain safe food handling practices with students.

School kitchens and other facilities that prepare and serve food to students on a larger scale must be registered and have control systems in place. However, this requirement does not apply to Home Economics classrooms used for educational purposes, where food is prepared by students for their own use rather than for sale or service to others. In municipal operations, it is common for one or more committees to act as food business operators, thereby bearing responsibility for ensuring compliance with food safety regulations (Swedish Association of Local Authorities and Regions, 2020).

Regarding Home Economics classrooms, the school's principal organiser (the municipality for public schools or the owner for independent schools) holds the overall responsibility for ensuring that hygiene practices adhere to current laws and guidelines. This means that the principal or school administration must ensure that the facilities and equipment in the HE classroom are in a condition that allows hygiene and safety regulations to be followed. However, the daily responsibility for ensuring that students comply with hygiene practices lies with the Home Economics teacher. The teacher must instruct and supervise students to ensure proper hygiene during cooking and other practical activities. This includes handwashing, correct handling of raw ingredients, and maintaining clean work surfaces and equipment.

2.3.1. The Food Act in the Home Economics Classroom

The Food Act (Livsmedelslagen, 2006:804) regulates various aspects of food handling, storage, production, and serving. The law partially applies to the Home Economics classroom in a school, as Home Economics classrooms cannot be classified as part of a private household according to EU food legislation or Swedish food law.

A private household, as defined by the Swedish Food Agency (Livsmedelsverket), refers to a group of people sharing a residence and being responsible for the household's food supply. This definition does not include school environments or classrooms, even if food is prepared and consumed there. Schools and their activities fall outside the concept of a "private household," meaning that food legislation requirements for hygiene and safety apply to school facilities, even though they are not run as commercial food businesses. However, the sections of the Food Act concerning food serving, production, and sales do not apply to the HE classroom.

Regarding work in the Home Economics classroom, the following aspects of the Food Act are relevant:

1. **Requirements for Food Safety:**
   The Food Act establishes overarching requirements for food safety. This means that food used in the Home Economics classroom must be handled in a way that ensures it is safe for consumption and does not pose a health risk to students. General food safety requirements include:

   a) *Hygiene:*
      Food must be handled in a way that prevents contamination and pollution. This means that everyone handling food must follow strict hygiene routines,

including handwashing, the use of protective clothing (aprons), and cleaning kitchen equipment and surfaces.

b) *Proper Storage:*
Food must be stored correctly to prevent the growth of harmful bacteria and deterioration of quality. This means that fresh food must be kept at an appropriate temperature, and frozen and refrigerated food must be stored according to the manufacturer's recommendations.

c) *Food Inspection:*
Food must be regularly inspected to ensure it is safe for consumption. This includes checking expiration dates, inspecting food for signs of spoilage, and following proper cooking methods.

d) *Allergen Management:*
Foods that can cause allergic reactions must be handled with extra care to prevent contamination. This includes informing about the presence of allergens in food and avoiding cross-contamination between different food items.

e) *Traceability:*
Food must be traceable back to its original source to enable quick and efficient recalls if necessary. This means that food must be properly labelled and stored.

2. **Handling and Storage of Food:**
Legislation sets requirements for how food should be handled and stored to minimise both the risk of contamination and spoilage. This includes hygiene requirements, cleaning of

kitchen equipment and surfaces, and proper storage of fresh, frozen, and cooked food.

3. **Food Establishments:**
   The Food Act also regulates requirements for food establishments, including kitchens and dining areas in schools and educational institutions. These establishments must meet specific hygiene and safety standards to be allowed to handle and serve food. Although Home Economics classrooms are not classified as food establishments under the law - where production for sale and serving to individuals other than those who prepared the food is regulated - they must still adhere to many of the same hygiene and safety requirements. This is because HE classrooms handle food during educational activities, making food safety and good hygiene practices essential to protect both students and teachers.

   The requirements for cleanliness, safe handling of ingredients, proper storage, and cooking apply here as well, even though the food is not served commercially or to external individuals. This ensures that students have a safe learning environment (as required by the Education Act) while also gaining practical experience in proper food handling procedures.

   Food Establishments according to The Food Act
   - *Good Hygiene Practices:*
     In the Home Economics classroom, good hygiene practices must be applied to prevent food contamination. This includes rules for personal hygiene of both staff and students, cleaning and disinfection of surfaces and equipment, pest control, and monitoring water quality.

- *Cleaning and Disinfection Procedures:*
  The teaching kitchen must have clear procedures for cleaning and disinfecting kitchen equipment, work surfaces, and other areas where food is handled to prevent cross-contamination and the spread of bacteria.

- *Staff Training:*
  Teachers and other staff involved in food handling and cooking must be properly trained in food safety and hygiene practices to minimise the risk of foodborne illnesses. Teaching activities should include accurate theoretical information on food hygiene and be adapted to the students' skill level and knowledge of food safety (in accordance with the core content of Lgr22).

- *Traceability:*
  All food establishments must have systems in place to trace food back to its original source.

- *Food Labelling:*
  Legislation also includes requirements for food labelling, meaning that food must be correctly labelled with information about ingredients, allergens, best-before dates, and other relevant details for both teachers and students.

- *HACCP System:*
  Food establishments should implement the Hazard Analysis and Critical Control Points (HACCP) system to identify, assess, and control food safety risks throughout the food production process. In Home Economics classrooms, this practice can be used for educational purposes (in accordance with Lgr22 and the subject's core content).

Hazard Analysis and Critical Control Points (HACCP)-system

In the systematic work environment management of the Home Economics classroom, the HACCP system can be adapted and used to enhance food safety while also following the recommendations in the Swedish Work Environment Authority's regulations regarding infection risks.

Section 5: The Swedish Work Environment Authority's regulations on systematic work environment management include rules requiring employers to regularly assess working conditions and evaluate potential risks in the workplace. The regulations also state that employers must take measures to prevent health hazards.

Swedish Work Environment Authority's provisions on Infection Risks 2018, AFS 2018:4

Section 7 states that in workplaces where there is a risk of infection, the employer must take measures to prevent the spread of infectious agents and ensure that the number of employees at risk of exposure is kept as low as possible. Additionally, Section 9 requires employers to ensure that employees working in environments with infection risks have access to handwashing or disinfection facilities. The key aspects of food safety and risk assessment focus on enabling good practices in an optimal environment.

In the Home Economics classroom, the application of the Hazard Analysis and Critical Control Points (HACCP) system can be integrated in various ways. Primarily, it concerns the teacher's approach, which should incorporate the HACCP method into daily work in the classroom. Including different aspects of HACCP in teaching requires the teacher to be knowledgeable about the system and its application, ensuring that it is implemented in practical teaching tasks. Several key areas of the subject are well suited for this, including hygiene and food safety in handling, cooking, and storing food, as well as routines and methods for cleaning and sanitation.

An inspirational image of HACCP System in Practice.
By E. Larsson/Artelinas.

HACCP System in Practice

It is possible to work with HACCP by focusing on kitchen hygiene and cooking temperatures, for example

1. *Identifying Different Types of Risks and Hazards (e.g., Salmonella):*
   Before cooking begins, the teacher and students can work together to identify potential hazards in the cooking process, such as cross-contamination, insufficient heating of food, and allergen handling.

2. *Hazard Assessment:*
   Once hazards have been identified, their potential risk to food safety is assessed. This includes evaluating how

likely a particular hazard is to occur and the consequences if it does.

3. *Determining Critical Control Points (CCP):*
   Critical control points in cooking can be identified, such as proper handling of raw ingredients, correct cooking temperatures, and appropriate storage methods. At each critical control point, specific measures can be established to minimise the risk of risks.

4. *Establishing Critical Limits for Each CCP:*
   For each Critical Control Point (CCP), specific limits can be set to ensure that food is prepared and handled safely. This includes maintaining specific temperatures during cooking and storage.
   For example, when preparing chicken nuggets, students should understand the importance of the different stages of double breading from a hygiene perspective:
   o Handling raw egg and raw chicken safely
   o Using separate cutting boards for different ingredients
   o Washing hands between steps
   o Properly cleaning utensils
   o Ensuring the food is thoroughly cooked

5. *Implementing a Monitoring System:*
   During cooking, a monitoring system can be established to ensure CCPs are controlled and critical limits are maintained. This may include regular temperature checks and visual food inspections (e.g., ensuring chicken reaches an internal temperature of at least 72°C).

6. *Defining Corrective Actions for Deviations:*
   If monitoring shows that critical limits are not being met at any CCP, corrective actions must be taken to address the issue and ensure food safety.

   For example, students may need to adjust their cooking methods during the process to achieve the proper food safety standards.

By incorporating the HACCP system into Home Economics studies, students have the opportunity to discover and understand the principles of food safety, hygiene, and risk management through hands-on experience with food in real-life situations.

Constructivist pedagogy stresses that students build their own knowledge through experience and active participation. When teachers integrate the HACCP system into daily classroom activities, students not only learn theoretical concepts, but also how to apply them in practice. For example, by working with hygiene and food safety in food handling, cooking, and storage, as well as following cleaning and sanitation routines, students develop a deeper understanding of how to identify and prevent risks in kitchen environments. They learn to think critically, recognise potential hazards, and make informed decisions about safe food handling, ensuring that their learning is strongly connected to real-world applications. This practical use of the HACCP system helps students bridge the gap between theory and practice, leading to a deeper understanding and the long-term development of essential life skills.

Furthermore, this approach enhances students' sense of responsibility and independence. By actively engaging in tasks that require reflection on safety routines and hygiene, they become more aware of potential risks in kitchen settings and how to manage them safely. This strengthens their ability to think systematically and apply critical thinking - key aspects of a constructivist learning environment, where students develop knowledge through interaction with their surroundings and hands-on tasks.

2.3.2. The Environmental Code and the Home Economics Studies Classroom

The planning and implementation of a Home Economics classroom can be linked to the Swedish Environmental Code (Miljöbalken, 1998:808) in several ways, particularly in relation to chemical handling, waste management, and health-related aspects. Health and safety considerations were previously discussed in the subsection on workplace safety. In practice, these considerations may include regulations on noise levels, ventilation, and the use of hazardous substances - all essential for designing a Home Economics classroom that ensures a safe and healthy working environment for both students and staff. This topic is further explored in *Book II, Material Framework for Home Economics*.

Although the Environmental Code is not the primary legislation governing activities in a Home Economics studies classroom, it may still be relevant in the areas mentioned above.

1. **Chemical Management:**
   The Environmental Code regulates the use, handling, and storage of chemicals to reduce risks to human health and the environment. In a Home Economics studies classroom, this may include the safe use and storage of cleaning agents, cooking ingredients, and other chemicals used in teaching. This topic is addressed in the Book III, *Structural Framework for Home Economics*.

   This section has been added to provide a broader perspective on the subject's content and its didactics, making it easier to understand. This part is not included in the Swedish version of the book.

   Shortly, In Sweden, the Environmental Code sets clear regulations for the use, handling, and storage of chemicals to protect human health and the environment. These regulations are particularly relevant in a Home Economics classroom, where various chemicals, such as cleaning agents and certain food additives, are used in teaching. To ensure a safe and sustainable learning environment, schools must follow strict storage and handling procedures. All chemicals should be clearly labelled according to EU regulations, such as the CLP (Classification, Labelling, and Packaging) Regulation, indicating any potential risks. Hazardous substances must be stored securely in well-ventilated, lockable cabinets, with incompatible substances, such as acids and bases, kept separate to prevent dangerous reactions.

Proper handling is equally important. Schools are required to conduct regular risk assessments of all chemicals used, in accordance with guidelines from the Swedish Work Environment Authority (Arbetsmiljöverket). When handling strong cleaning agents or hazardous substances, appropriate personal protective equipment, such as gloves and safety goggles, should be worn. Students should only handle potentially dangerous substances under supervision, following clear instructions. To minimise environmental impact, schools are encouraged to use non-toxic and eco-friendly alternatives whenever possible, following recommendations from the Swedish Chemicals Agency (Kemikalieinspektionen). Chemical waste must be disposed of responsibly, adhering to municipal waste management regulations, rather than being poured down drains.

Finally, emergency preparedness is essential. Classrooms must be equipped with eye wash stations, spill kits, fire extinguishers, and proper ventilation to handle potential accidents. Any chemical-related incidents should be documented and reported according to school safety protocols. By applying these practices,

Swedish schools ensure that Home Economics classrooms comply with national regulations while promoting a safe, healthy, and environmentally responsible learning environment.

2. **Waste Management:**
    The Environmental Code includes provisions on how waste should be managed and sorted to promote recycling and minimise environmental impact. Schools are required to comply with these regulations and ensure that waste from the HE classroom is handled in an environmentally responsible manner. This topic is addressed in the *Book III, Structural Framework for Home Economics.*

    The Environmental Code sets clear guidelines for waste management, emphasising recycling and reducing environmental impact. Schools are required to follow these regulations to ensure that waste from the Home Economics classroom is handled responsibly. Proper waste sorting and disposal are key components of sustainable waste management. Schools must separate waste into designated categories, such as food waste, packaging, paper, plastics, and hazardous materials, in accordance with municipal waste management regulations. Organic waste from cooking activities should be composted or collected for biogas production, while recyclable materials should be properly sorted to support Sweden's circular economy goals.

    To further reduce environmental impact, schools are encouraged to implement waste reduction strategies, such as minimising food waste through careful meal planning, reusing materials where possible, and opting for sustainable products. Clear waste disposal instructions should be provided to students to promote environmentally responsible habits. Additionally, hazardous waste, such as expired cleaning agents or used cooking oil, must be handled according to specific safety and environmental guidelines to prevent contamination. Schools are responsible for ensuring that such waste is disposed of at appropriate collection points. By following these practices, Home Economics classrooms contribute to Sweden's ambitious environmental goals, fostering a culture of sustainability and responsible resource management.

2.3.3. Local Governing Documents

Municipalities or schools may also establish governing documents related to food and health, such as a public health plan or a meal policy. Food and cooking in schools involve multiple stakeholders and extend beyond school meals to include all aspects of food handling and preparation in Home Economics classrooms. Therefore, it is essential that these matters are carefully planned and adapted to meet the specific conditions and needs of each organisation.

Public Health Plan and Meal Policy Program

Most municipalities outline their public health goals in a long-term public health plan, which is typically based on the national public health policy adopted by the Swedish Parliament. The overarching public health goal in Sweden is to create conditions for good health on equal terms for the entire population (Public Health Agency of Sweden, Folkhälsomyndigheten, 2022d). Fundamentally, this involves establishing a structural framework that supports national efforts to promote health and reduce health inequalities within society. The Public Health Agency of Sweden has been tasked by the government to develop this framework, which focuses on integrating national objectives, and engaging various government agencies to advance health equity. This also includes defining indicators to measure progress in different health areas, including specific indicators to monitor health equality.

Several studies have shown that health inequalities persist when certain social groups experience systematic differences in health based on their socioeconomic status. These disparities are not random but follow a clear trend, where health gradually declines along the social hierarchy (Public Health Agency of Sweden, Folkhälsomyndigheten, 2022d). The most vulnerable groups, particularly those facing social and economic disadvantages, are disproportionately affected by health problems compared to others.

Today's health disparities stem from both historical and contemporary factors. Achieving good and equitable health requires long-term efforts to improve the underlying conditions for health, combined with short-term measures to mitigate the immediate consequences of unequal health determinants.

*Public Health Agency of Sweden
(Folkhälsomyndigheten), 2022d*

Teaching Home Economics studies plays a crucial role in promoting equal knowledge about a healthy lifestyle. When it comes to food, this aligns with goal areas 1 and 6 of the national public health policy: Conditions during early life and Lifestyle habits (Folkhälsomyndigheten, 2022d). Achieving these goals requires efforts from multiple stakeholders.

Many municipalities have a meal policy program or a meal policy as a tool to support these objectives. Such programs may also include municipal decisions on the government's goals and strategies for organic production and consumption, as well as measures to reduce food waste and minimise the environmental impact of meals (Sigtuna Kommun, 2018; Katrineholm Kommun, 2024). Beyond defining goals and ambitions, it is essential to clarify responsibilities and establish a follow-up plan. A meal policy can help outline objectives in areas such as meal quality (e.g., ensuring meals are nutritious, environmentally sustainable, safe, enjoyable, and well integrated) and organisation (e.g., competence, authority, and division of responsibilities).

Meal Policy in Practice

A meal policy for a school in Sweden can serve multiple purposes and be based on various underlying values and principles. When developing such a policy, different aspects may be highlighted - for example, a focus on sustainability or nutritional quality. In these cases, factors such as locally sourced ingredients and the climate impact of food may form the foundation of the policy (Mattanken, 2024). A meal or food policy for a school can include several key components (cf. Katrineholm Kommun, 2024; Strömstad Kommun, 2022; Sigtuna Kommun, 2018), many of which can also be incorporated into meals prepared in Home Economics studies:

- **Food Quality and Health**
  A food and meal policy can establish guidelines to promote healthy eating among students. It may include recommendations or requirements for providing nutritious and balanced meals in schools. Additionally, the policy can highlight the use of fresh, locally sourced, and organic ingredients whenever possible (Katrineholm Kommun, 2024).

- **Enjoyable Meals in a Pleasant Environment**
  A meal policy can also focus on ensuring that schools offer flavourful meals in an inviting setting. This could involve providing a variety of spices and condiments, allowing students to adjust flavours according to their preferences. A pleasant meal environment means creating a space where students feel comfortable and welcome while eating (Strömstad Kommun, 2022). Key factors include cleanliness, a positive atmosphere, comfortable seating, and opportunities for social interaction during meals.

- **Sustainability**
  A meal policy can emphasise the importance of sustainability and environmental awareness in school meals. This may include guidelines for reducing food waste, promoting recycling of packaging, and encouraging the use of local and organic ingredients (Sigtuna Kommun, 2018). Such a policy can also encourage students to choose vegetarian or vegan options and reduce meat consumption for environmental reasons (Katrineholm Kommun, 2024).

- **Allergy and Hygiene Management (Safe Meals)**
  A meal policy may include guidelines for managing food allergies and dietary restrictions among students. Schools must be aware of students' allergies and take them into account when preparing and serving meals. The policy may also recommend avoiding common allergens in the school cafeteria.

  Additionally, the policy outlines essential hygiene and food safety measures to ensure that all meals are safe to consume. This includes

  > *"using verified cooking methods in school kitchens and ensuring that kitchen staff responsible for preparing and serving food comply with current legislation to guarantee food safety."*

  Strömstad Kommun, 2022

- **Food-Related Routines**
  A meal policy can establish routines for school meals, including lunch, snacks, and breakfast schedules. It may also provide guidelines on the time allocated for eating, specify which types of food are allowed to be brought and consumed at school, and outline procedures for food waste management (Katrineholm Kommun, 2024).

- **Education and Awareness**
  A meal policy often includes educational components to raise awareness about health, nutrition, and dietary habits. Schools can integrate nutrition education into the curriculum and provide informational materials and events for students and parents. This initiative can also be incorporated into Home Economics studies, reinforcing its relevance in daily life.

A well-structured and effectively implemented meal policy aims to create a healthy and sustainable food environment for students while promoting long-term healthy eating habits. Additionally, it supports equity in healthy lifestyles by accommodating students with special dietary needs and increasing awareness of food's impact on both health and the environment.

An inspiring image of a HE classroom,
featuring a design that blends workplace safety with functionality.
By E. Larsson, created using a graphic design program
and IKEA's planning tool.

*All students must be guaranteed a learning environment where
education is characterised by safety and teaching by a sense of
calm and focus.*

The Swedish Education Act, (Skollagen 2010:800)

2.4. Risk Assessment and Risk Management

Risk Assessment and Workplace Safety Responsibility

The Swedish Work Environment Authority's regulations on occupational safety for minors apply to all students within the Swedish education system, ensuring that children and young people are protected from potential hazards in school environments. These regulations aim to create a safe and healthy learning atmosphere, minimising risks associated with practical lessons, school facilities, and other educational activities. A minor student is defined as any student from preschool class (grade zero) until the completion of their education, but no later than the age of 18. This definition includes students in both compulsory and upper secondary education. Since students frequently engage in hands-on activities, there is a need for structured risk assessments and preventive measures to safeguard their well-being.

The responsibility for risk assessment and workplace safety lies primarily with the municipality, which oversees the administration of public schools. This responsibility is typically delegated to the principal within municipal school boards, who must ensure that all safety protocols are in place and followed. However, in practice, this responsibility may also be assigned to specific school staff members, such as lead teachers in subjects that involve potential hazards. The Swedish Work Environment Authority provides guidelines to help schools manage these risks effectively (Arbetsmiljöverket, 2013).

In independent schools, which operate outside municipal governance, the principal authority follows similar practices as municipal school boards. The principal is generally responsible for conducting risk assessments before any modifications to school operations or when potential risks are identified. These assessments ensure that students and staff are not exposed to unnecessary dangers. In some cases, the responsibility for risk assessment may be delegated to subject-specific teachers, such as those overseeing chemistry or woodworking classes, due to their expertise in handling hazardous materials and equipment. When this delegation occurs, the principal must ensure that the assigned teachers possess the necessary competence to assess risks accurately and implement safety measures effectively. Additionally, they must be given sufficient time and resources to carry out these assessments properly, preventing safety checks from being rushed or overlooked. Schools are expected to maintain ongoing evaluations of their risk management procedures, adapting to new challenges and ensuring continuous compliance with safety regulations. Ultimately, these occupational safety regulations serve to protect students and create an environment where learning can take place without unnecessary risks. By assigning clear responsibilities to school leadership and staff, the Swedish education system aims to uphold high standards of safety and well-being for all students.

Risk Assessment and Preventive Measures

An essential aspect of workplace safety is risk assessment and management. Schools should conduct a thorough risk assessment of the Home Economics classroom to identify potential hazards and evaluate risks for both students and staff. These risks may include cuts, burns, slip accidents, and allergic reactions to food. The Home Economics teacher plays a key role in conducting and participating in risk assessments.

As a trained expert in the subject's broad content, the teacher is responsible for leading activities and exercises that prioritise student safety, particularly in the kitchen or when using various tools and equipment. This role is especially important in practical instruction, where students engage in potentially hazardous tasks involving kitchen equipment, sharp knives, and hot surfaces or materials. The teacher must ensure that students understand and follow safety regulations and that appropriate protective measures are in place to minimise risks. Additionally, the teacher is responsible for planning tasks safely, ensuring that students have the necessary knowledge to work with the required methods and tools.

Contact Materials

Several laws regulate materials and products intended to come into contact with food. Regulation (EC) No. 1935/2004 concerns materials and products designed for food contact. In addition, there are more specific regulations for certain materials, as well as Regulation (EC) No. 2023/2006 on good manufacturing practices. Those responsible for selecting materials in a Home Economics studies classroom should be aware of the various properties of materials used in practical work.

According to the Swedish Food Agency (Livsmedelsverket, 2023b), contact materials include all materials intended to come into contact with food, such as:

- Food packaging materials, including plastic bags, plastic films, paper bags, cardboard and plastic packaging, and various types of foil.
- Tableware, such as porcelain, glass, and cutlery.
- Kitchen utensils, including pots, frying pans, baking trays, ladles, and whisks.
- Kitchen appliances, such as coffee makers and electric mixers.
- Parts of cooking appliances, such as seals and hoses.

Products designed for food contact, such as spatulas or immersion blenders; do not require an official approval marking for food use. However, there are different ways to indicate that a product is safe for food contact. A commonly used symbol is the "glass and fork" mark, which confirms that the product is safe to use with food under normal conditions. If the material has any limitations, such as temperature restrictions, this information should be displayed alongside the symbol. Another way to indicate food safety is by explicitly stating "for food contact" or specifying the intended use, such as "Milk Jug."

Municipal Responsibility for Preventive Measures Against Accidents

---

1 § To protect human life, health, property, and the environment, the municipality must ensure that measures are taken to prevent fires and damage caused by fires. Additionally, without limiting the responsibilities of others, the municipality must work to provide protection against other types of accidents beyond fires.

The Act on Protection Against Accidents
(Lag om skydd mot olyckor, 2003:778)

In practice, this means that the municipality is responsible for preventing fires and other accidents to protect human life, health, property, and the environment. In the context of Home Economics studies, this responsibility may require the municipality, in collaboration with the school and other relevant parties, to implement measures that ensure a safe and healthy working environment for both students and staff. In the HE classroom, this includes several practical measures:

- **Risk assessment:**
  Conducting regular risk assessments to identify and address potential hazards in the HE classroom, such as slip accidents, fires, or cuts.

- **Routine inspections of tools and kitchen appliances:**
  Ensuring that all kitchen equipment in the HE classroom is in proper working order to prevent accidents caused by malfunctioning tools or appliances.

- **Cleaning and maintenance of kitchen equipment:**
  Regular upkeep and cleaning to prevent accidents resulting from faulty or poorly maintained kitchen appliances.

- **Safety Training:**
  Conducting training and providing information for students and staff on the safe use of kitchen equipment, handling hazardous substances, and administering first aid in case of accidents or incidents.

- **Fire Prevention:**
  Implementing fire safety measures and procedures to prevent fires, such as proper use of kitchen equipment, monitoring stoves and ovens, and storing flammable materials safely.

- **Emergency Evacuation Plans:**
  Establishing and practicing emergency evacuation plans to ensure that students and staff know how to respond in case of an accident or emergency in the HE classroom.

The Swedish Civil Contingencies Agency (MSB) is responsible for ensuring that municipalities comply with laws and regulations related to safety and preparedness, including those concerning fire prevention and accident prevention measures. This means that MSB oversees municipalities to ensure they maintain safety standards and follow the guidelines and requirements established to protect human life, health, property, and the environment.

County administrative boards also play a role by providing information about local and regional conditions to support MSB's work when needed.

---

1 a § The Swedish Civil Contingencies Agency (MSB) shall oversee that municipalities comply with this law and related regulations. County administrative boards shall, upon request, provide information about local and regional conditions.

The Act on Protection Against Accidents
(Lag om skydd mot olyckor, 2003:778)

Many provisions in the Swedish Work Environment Authority's regulations on the work environment for minors carry legal penalties (Swedish Work Environment Authority, 2013). The authority has the power to prohibit certain types of work if specific conditions are not met or to require an employer to take corrective measures.

As the principal authority of a school, one holds both work environment responsibility and criminal liability. Work environment responsibility involves implementing measures to prevent workplace hazards, while criminal liability means that a court determines who is accountable if an accident occurs. It is not possible to internally assign or negotiate criminal liability within an organisation. However, the court considers how responsibilities and tasks have been structured within the organisation, as well as whether an individual had sufficient authority, financial resources, and competence to fulfil their obligations.

Sometimes you have a messier group and feel like you don't have full control over knives, hot ovens, etc. I have also had suspended students come into Home Economics because, of course, they should have the "fun" lessons—

despite the fact that we have knives and other equipment. There have been occasions when I have felt afraid in these situations, both for my own safety and for the safety of other students.

Survey 2020

The teacher's comment highlights several workplace safety concerns in Home Economics classrooms, particularly regarding security and risk management. Survey responses from 2020, 2021, 2022, and 2024 indicate that teachers sometimes feel unsafe, especially when managing disruptive student groups or students who have been suspended from lessons but still participate in practical activities involving dangerous tools, such as knives and hot ovens. This creates an unsafe work environment where teachers fear for both their own safety and that of their students.

This sense of insecurity is closely tied to the employer's responsibility for the work environment, as outlined in the Swedish Work Environment Authority's regulations. The teacher suggests that safety issues arise due to a lack of control over the situation, posing a real risk of accidents. Since schools hold criminal liability if an incident occurs, it becomes evident that preventive measures - such as ensuring a safe learning environment and maintaining classroom order - do not always function effectively in practice. This underscores the importance of school leadership establishing clear procedures and rules to handle potentially dangerous situations, as well as providing teachers with the necessary resources and authority to create a safe and secure work environment.

Infection Transmission

Infection transmission can occur through food and human contact (cf. Arbetsmiljöverket, 2018:4).

1. **Infection Transmission via Food**

   Infection transmission via food occurs when disease-causing microorganisms are transferred to humans through contaminated food. These microorganisms can originate from raw ingredients, unclean surfaces, or individuals handling the food. Transmission happens when food is not handled or prepared hygienically, potentially leading to food poisoning or other foodborne illnesses.

   Regulation (EC) No 852/2004 and its Annexes I and II outline general hygiene requirements for all food-handling businesses, including schools and Home Economics classrooms. By adhering to these fundamental requirements - covering facilities, equipment, hygiene procedures, and staff training - schools can implement effective preventive measures and maintain a safe working environment in Home Economics classrooms. Proper control over these key conditions helps reduce the risk of infection transmission.

Inspections

Inspections can be conducted by the Home Economics teacher, in collaboration with the school's janitor or other staff members. According to the Swedish Food Agency (Livsmedelsverket), several key areas can serve as the foundation for internal inspections, including:

- *Staff training*
- *Personal hygiene*
- *Facility premises, equipment, and maintenance*
- *Cleaning*
- *Pest control*
- *Temperature monitoring*
- *Water quality*
- *Goods reception*
- *Food information: labelling, integrity*
- *Traceability*
- *Microbiological and chemical criteria*

Livsmedelsverket, 2021b

---

2. Infection Transmission Between Humans

Infection transmission between humans occurs when disease-causing microorganisms are transferred directly from one person to another through close contact or via airborne particles. This can happen through coughing, sneezing, or sharing contaminated objects, such as handshakes. Human-to-human transmission is common with airborne diseases like colds, influenza, and COVID-19, but it can also include other illnesses spread through bodily fluids or direct contact.

The Swedish Work Environment Authority (Arbetsmiljöverket, 2023b) has provided recommendations on measures to reduce the risk of infection transmission in schools:

- *Implement technical and organisational measures to reduce infection transmission.*
- *Ensure that soap, paper towels, and hand sanitiser are available in multiple locations throughout the school.*
- *Maintain good air quality.*
- *Inform staff and students on how to act if they start feeling unwell during the school day.*
- *Ensure that all premises are thoroughly cleaned. Frequently touched surfaces, such as door handles, light switches, keyboards, and tablets, should be cleaned regularly.*
- *Encourage outdoor activities.*

Arbetsmiljöverket, 2023b

2.4.1. Fire Safety

An inspiring image of a modern HE classroom
featuring fire-safe materials and an open-plan design.
By E. Larsson, created using a graphic design program and IKEA's planning tool.

The Fire safety regulations in Swedish schools are outlined in various laws, ordinances, and directives. The most important ones concerning fire safety in school buildings are the Act on Protection Against Accidents (SFS 2003:778) and the Swedish National Board of Housing, Building, and Planning's Building Regulations, in Swedish Boverkets byggregler (BBR).

1. **Act on Protection Against Accidents (2003:778)**

    This law regulates accident prevention and may include provisions on fire safety and fire prevention measures in school buildings.

---

1 § To protect human life and health, as well as property and the environment, municipalities must ensure that measures are taken to prevent fires and fire-related damages. Additionally, without limiting the responsibility of others, they must work to provide protection against other types of accidents beyond fires.

2 Chap. 2§ – Owners or tenants of buildings or other facilities must, to a reasonable extent, maintain equipment for fire extinguishing and life-saving in the event of a fire or other accidents. They must also take necessary measures to prevent fires and to limit or prevent damage caused by fire.

The Act on Protection Against Accidents
(Lag om skydd mot olyckor, 2003:778)

This law also establishes regulations for fire protection in various types of buildings, including schools. According to the Swedish Civil Contingencies Agency (MSB, 2022), fire safety can be improved in many ways, including securing school buildings and their surroundings. For example, low roofs should be fireproofed, wooden sheds should be relocated, and alarms and sprinklers should be installed. Measures can also be taken to reduce the risk of arson, such as ensuring proper lighting and keeping bushes and hedges low.

2. Swedish National Board of Housing, Building, and Planning's Building Regulations (BBR)

The Swedish National Board of Housing, Building, and Planning (Boverket), the national authority responsible for building and housing regulations, has published building codes that include fire protection requirements for buildings (Boverket, 2023). The Building The Building Regulations (BBR) are based on the fundamental provisions of the Planning and Building Act (2010:900) and its associated ordinance, the Planning and Building Ordinance (2011:338). Fire safety regulations are further developed and clarified in Section 5 of the BBR, which contains binding provisions and general recommendations.

BBR includes detailed requirements and guidelines for construction, evacuation, fire alarms, fire suppression, and other fire safety measures in school environments. For example, Boverket's regulations on the fire properties of floors and walls are outlined in BBR 2008, Chapter 5 (Fire Protection). Fire safety requirements are determined by the building's fire classification (1–3) and the specific type of space. Most school buildings fall into Fire Class 1 or Fire Class 2.

Regarding fire safety in a Home Economics classroom, regulations and guidelines assume that the building is designed, constructed, and equipped to minimize the risk of fire. This principle should also be applied when selecting surface materials, furniture, and equipment for the Home Economics study area. For instance, it is recommended that interior textiles in classrooms meet Fire Class SL 1, which indicates resistance to ignition.

Fire Safety in the Home Economics Classroom

In Swedish school buildings, specific regulations and guidelines apply to fire safety (Swedish Fire Protection Association, Svenska Brandskyddsföreningen, 2023). Several key preventive measures are essential in schools and particularly in Home Economics classrooms:

1. **Fire Alarm:**
   - All school buildings must be equipped with a functional fire alarm.
   - The alarm system should be connected to a monitoring centre capable of taking necessary actions in case of fire.
   - In a HE classroom, the alarm unit and its placement should be adapted to the use of ovens and dishwashers to prevent false alarms.

2. **Fire Extinguishing Equipment:**
   - Adequate fire extinguishing equipment must be placed in an easily accessible location within the classroom.
   - In the HE classroom, the fire safety equipment should be clearly visible and properly labelled.
   - The initial fire extinguishing equipment should include:
     - A fire blanket (minimum size: 150 cm x 180 cm).
     - A fire extinguisher.

3. **Evacuation Routes:**
   - All school buildings must have clearly marked and unobstructed evacuation routes.
   - In a HE classroom, evacuation routes must be highly visible, free from obstructions such as furniture or other objects, and easily accessible and usable in an emergency.

4. **Emergency Lighting:**
Emergency lighting must be installed along evacuation routes to facilitate evacuation in the event of a power outage or poor visibility due to smoke.

5. **Fire Safety Training and Evacuation Procedures:**
   - All school staff and students should be trained in fire prevention measures and how to respond in case of a fire. Training should include fire extinguishing techniques, evacuation routes, and how to alert the fire department.
   - In the HE classroom, students must follow specific evacuation procedures, such as:
     - Turning off stove burners and ovens before evacuating.
     - Walking quickly but calmly through the designated evacuation route to the assembly point.
   - The teacher is responsible for:
     - Turning off the main power switch.
     - Ensuring all students have exited before leaving the classroom.

6. **Fire Drills:**
School administration should regularly conduct fire drills and safety reviews to ensure that all students and staff are familiar with fire procedures and can respond appropriately in an emergency.

7. **Fire Doors and Firewalls:**
Certain areas within school buildings may require fire doors and firewalls to prevent the spread of fire and smoke. These areas must remain locked when not in use to prevent unauthorised access.

2.4.2. Threats, Violence, and Harassment

Violence refers to intentional harm inflicted on another person, which can be psychological, physical, or material. The threat of violence has no place in a safe learning and working environment. Workplace violence includes any violent situation that arises in relation to work duties, involving an employee (e.g., a teacher) and a customer (e.g., a student) or between employees. In this context, the term employee refers to teachers, students, and other school staff.

Several laws and regulations govern threats and violence in Swedish schools. The most important legal frameworks relevant to working in a Home Economics classroom include:

1. **The Education Act (Skollag 2010:800):**
   The Education Act is the primary legislation governing education in Sweden. It includes provisions on safety and order during Home Economics lessons. The law emphasises that students must be able to study and interact in a safe and secure environment, and that preventive measures must be taken to address threats and violence.

2. **Work Environment Legislation:**
   The Work Environment Act and the Swedish Work Environment Authority's regulations on systematic work environment management (Systematiskt arbetsmiljöarbete, 2001:1) are essential in protecting school staff from threats and violence. The employer is responsible for implementing systematic work environment management, which includes risk assessments and measures to prevent and handle threats and violence in the school environment.

3. **The Discrimination Act (Diskrimineringslagen, 2008:567):**
   The Discrimination Act prohibits discrimination and harassment based on gender, ethnicity, religion, disability, sexual orientation, or similar circumstances. This law applies to the school environment, including HE classrooms, aiming to create an inclusive and safe space for both students and staff.

4. **Crimes Against Individuals:**
   Crimes such as threats, violence, or assault fall under Swedish criminal law (Brottsbalken 1962:700). If threats or violence occur in a school setting, a police report can be filed, and actions may be taken according to criminal law.

   In Home Economics lessons,

   - Threats (Chapter 4, Section 5) refer to intimidation directed at another person.
   - Assault (Chapter 3, Section 5) includes inflicting bodily harm or pain on another individual.

The Swedish Education Act includes provisions regulating violence and threats in the school environment, including during Home Economics lessons. According to the Education Act, schools are obligated to provide a safe and secure environment for students and staff. In practice, this means schools must prevent and counteract degrading treatment, harassment, violence, and threats by implementing measures to ensure a protected environment.

Students must follow the school's rules of conduct, which generally prohibit threats or violence against other students or staff. Violating school rules may lead to disciplinary actions by the school. Schools have the authority to impose such measures on students who breach the rules, including warnings, relocations, suspensions, or other actions to maintain a safe and secure environment for all.

According to the Education Act, school staff are required to report and investigate incidents, meaning they must notify the principal if they become aware of or suspect a student is experiencing degrading treatment, harassment, violence, or threats. The principal is then responsible for investigating the incident and taking appropriate measures. Schools must also take concrete action in cases of threats and violence. If a student engages in violence or threats against others, the school must respond swiftly and effectively. This may involve supporting and protecting the victim while also taking disciplinary action against the perpetrator. Schools are also required to inform and consult with students' guardians regarding any actions taken due to their behaviour. Furthermore, the school must offer support to all students involved in incidents of threats or violence, both to assist them and to help prevent future occurrences.

The school should proactively prevent threats and violence by fostering a safe, inclusive environment for all students and staff. This includes conflict resolution education, promoting positive behaviour, and setting clear rules and procedures for managing conflicts. According to the Education Act, failure to take adequate measures to prevent or address violence and threats may result in liability for damages to affected students or staff. A clear action plan and procedures for handling violence and threats - including during Home Economics lessons - are essential to help create a safe, supportive environment where students can learn and thrive.

The Teacher's and Student's Perspectives

Threats, violence, and degrading treatment during Home Economics lessons can be viewed from both student and teacher perspectives. From the student's perspective, several factors come into play. Students may face threats and violence from classmates, including physical assaults, verbal threats, or bullying related to performance, appearance, or personal traits. Such situations create an unsafe environment, harming students' well-being and learning. Students may also face discrimination and degrading treatment, such as derogatory comments, ridicule, or exclusion based on gender, ethnicity, religion, sexual orientation, or other factors. These experiences can negatively affect self-esteem, confidence, motivation, and participation in class activities (cf. Public Health Agency of Sweden, Folkhälsomyndigheten 2022c).

A lack of security and respect in the classroom often leads to an unsafe learning environment. If students feel threatened or afraid, their ability to focus and learn suffers. Such situations compromise students' right to a safe and inclusive learning environment and may lead to serious psychological effects (Sonmark & Modin, 2017). This can result in anxiety, sadness, low self-esteem, and reduced interest in school and the subject. Students may also feel isolated and lonely if they are afraid to share their experiences with teachers or other adults. Without proper support and intervention, affected students may feel abandoned and powerless.

Schools must establish clear procedures for handling and preventing such situations. Teachers and staff must remain vigilant and proactive in addressing issues. To create a safe and inclusive learning environment, schools should teach respect and empathy, enforce strict anti-bullying policies, and support affected students (Gustafsson, Allodi Westling, Åkerman, Eriksson, Eriksson, Fischbein, et al., 2010).

Threats, violence, and degrading treatment in Swedish schools present serious and complex challenges. From a teacher's perspective, multiple challenges arise. Some Home Economics teachers report facing threats, violence, and harassment at work. A 2022 survey found that 8.2% of teachers felt constantly or nearly constantly unsafe due to threats, violence, and harassment. By 2024, this figure had risen to 8.6%. Teachers may experience such behaviour from students, parents, or others in the school community, including verbal threats, physical assaults, online harassment, or other forms of degrading treatment. All the surveys from 2020 to 2024 show that these incidents harm teachers' well-being, work environment, and teaching effectiveness.

Teachers frequently handle student conflicts involving threats or violence, which can range from verbal altercations and intimidation to physical aggression. In addition to de-escalating these situations, they must manage and prevent conflicts while teaching students constructive, nonviolent conflict-resolution skills. However, effectively addressing such issues requires both training and support from school leadership, as many teachers feel unprepared to handle escalating conflicts on their own. Beyond direct conflicts between students, many teachers struggle with a broader issue: a perceived decline in respect for classroom rules and their authority. This can manifest in various ways, including verbal harassment, defiance, or passive resistance to instructions. Some students may openly challenge teachers through rude remarks, interruptions, or refusal to participate in lessons, while others express their disregard more subtly - through dismissive attitudes, eye-rolling, or ignoring directives. Such behaviour not only disrupts the learning environment but can also erode a teacher's confidence and sense of professional worth.

Moreover, teachers often face personal attacks that go beyond mere disobedience. Incidents such as derogatory comments, ridicule, and insults can take a significant emotional toll, affecting not just their self-esteem but also their ability to teach effectively. When a teacher feels disrespected or undermined, their motivation, engagement, and enthusiasm for teaching may wane, leading to a decline in instruction quality. Over time, this can contribute to increased stress, burnout, and even a reluctance to remain in the profession. The overall classroom atmosphere is also at stake. A lack of respect for teachers fosters a negative learning environment where students feel emboldened to challenge authority, and their peers may follow suit. If not properly addressed, this can create a cycle in which misbehaviour becomes normalised, making it increasingly difficult to restore discipline and mutual respect. As a result, both teachers and students suffer – teachers experience frustration and job dissatisfaction, while students miss the opportunity to learn in a structured, respectful, and supportive setting.

Research from 2020 to 2024 underscores the pressing need for clearer policies and stronger institutional support to empower teachers in Home Economics. When faced with threats, violence, and harassment, teachers often lack the necessary tools and guidance to respond effectively, leaving them vulnerable and under significant pressure. The absence of structured protocols not only increases uncertainty in critical situations but also contributes to a sense of isolation, where teachers feel they must navigate these challenges alone. Moreover, inadequate training and limited resources exacerbate the issue, making it difficult for educators to maintain a sense of safety and control in their classrooms. Chronic exposure to hostile behaviour can take a serious toll, leading to emotional exhaustion, diminished job satisfaction, and even long-term psychological distress. Many teachers report experiencing heightened anxiety, persistent stress, and in severe cases, symptoms of burnout or depression. This not only affects their personal well-being but also undermines their ability to foster a positive and engaging learning environment for students.

Left unaddressed, these challenges can have far-reaching consequences. Some teachers take prolonged sick leave to recover from the mental and emotional strain, while others consider leaving the profession entirely (based on research conducted between 2020 and 2024). A high turnover rate among educators not only disrupts students' learning but also places additional strain on remaining staff, creating a cycle that is difficult to break. To combat these issues, schools and educational authorities must implement targeted strategies that prioritise teacher safety and well-being. This includes comprehensive training programs on conflict resolution and crisis management, clear and enforceable policies for handling threats and violence, and robust support systems such as counselling and peer mentorship. Additionally, fostering a school culture rooted in respect, inclusivity, and accountability is essential to preventing such incidents from occurring in the first place. Proactive measures are key to creating an environment where both teachers and students feel secure, respected, and equipped to thrive.

"Ongoing Deadly Violence"

"Ongoing deadly violence" refers to incidents involving an immediate and serious threat to the lives and safety of students and staff. These situations often escalate rapidly and unpredictably, highlighting the need for schools to implement well-prepared strategies. Preventive measures, training, and clear emergency protocols can significantly improve response times and minimise potential harm. PDV, or *Pågående Dödligt Våld* (Ongoing Deadly Violence), is a police term used to describe violent acts intended to cause serious harm or death (Swedish Civil Contingencies Agency, Myndigheten för samhällsskydd och beredskap, MSB, 2024). Such acts are typically premeditated and carried out indiscriminately, often targeting individuals at random within a specific location.

While these incidents are rare, their potential consequences make it essential for schools and authorities to be thoroughly prepared for worst-case scenarios. The tragic school shooting at Campus Risbergska in Örebro on February 4, 2025 (Polisen, 2025), in which eleven people lost their lives, highlights the importance of schools and authorities being prepared for worst-case scenarios. To enhance safety, schools have to establish and regularly update their emergency preparedness plans, conduct training exercises, and ensure that both staff and students are aware of appropriate actions to take in crises. This includes lockdown procedures, evacuation plans, and effective communication channels with the police and emergency services. Promoting a school environment that prioritises mental health, early intervention, and conflict resolution strategies is also crucial in preventing such incidents.

Effective preparation requires not only clear protocols but also well-established best practices that can be consistently implemented and refined over time. Schools should establish and regularly update emergency action plans, conduct frequent training exercises, and ensure that both staff and students are well versed in appropriate response strategies. This includes lockdown procedures, evacuation plans, and effective communication channels with law enforcement and emergency responders. Regular drills and scenario-based training can help familiarise staff and students with emergency protocols, reducing panic and improving response efficiency in critical situations. Furthermore, fostering a school environment that prioritises mental health support, early intervention, and conflict resolution strategies is essential in both preventing such incidents and ensuring a swift, coordinated response when necessary.

By implementing proactive measures and ensuring a high level of preparedness, schools can create a safer environment where students and staff feel secure, even in the face of potential threats.

1. **Activation of Emergency Procedures**
   The school must have clear protocols for handling ongoing deadly violence situations. This includes the rapid activation of alarm systems and communication channels to alert staff and students of the danger. These systems must also be adapted for the HE classroom.

2. **Evacuation or Hiding**
   Depending on the situation, the school may need to quickly evacuate students and staff to a safe location outside the school. If safe evacuation is not possible, staff must instruct students to hide in secure locations within the school and remain silent to avoid drawing attention.

3. **Contacting Emergency Services and Police**
   The school must immediately contact emergency services and the police to report the situation and receive professional assistance and guidance.

4. **Implementation of Security Protocols and Training**
   It is essential for schools to have security protocols in place and ensure that staff undergo training to handle ongoing deadly violence situations. This may include simulations and drills to enhance staff preparedness and response capability in a real emergency.

5. **Protection of Students and Staff**
   The school must take measures to protect students and staff from danger. This may involve securing doors, blocking entrances, or using other physical protective measures to prevent the attacker from gaining access to the school.

Lockdown and Evacuation

Lockdown and evacuation are two different safety measures that can be implemented to handle various threats or dangers within the school building (Swedish Civil Contingencies Agency, Myndigheten för samhällsskydd och beredskap, 2024).

Lockdown:

- A lockdown means that students and staff remain inside the school building, staying in their classrooms or other secure locations.
- Lockdowns can be used as a safety measure in response to external threats, such as dangerous individuals or severe weather conditions.
- The purpose of a lockdown is to protect students and staff by keeping them safe and away from external threats.

Evacuation:

- Evacuation means that students and staff quickly and safely leave the school building and move to an external assembly point.
- Evacuation is typically used in response to internal threats or dangers within the school, such as fire, gas leaks, or ongoing deadly violence.
- The purpose of evacuation is to remove students and staff from danger and bring them to a safe location outside the school building, where they can wait for further instructions or assistance from emergency responders.

Summary

Home Economics studies is a unique school subject that requires specific structural and material conditions for effective instruction. Unlike many other subjects, it integrates theoretical knowledge with hands-on practical application, placing significant demands on both physical resources and pedagogical tools. To ensure a safe and functional learning environment, Home Economics classrooms must be equipped with well-planned and properly maintained kitchen facilities, including appliances, lighting, electricity, water, and drainage. Additionally, access to essential teaching materials - such as food supplies, textbooks, and digital resources - is crucial for delivering high-quality instruction.

Surveys conducted in 2020, 2021, 2022, and 2024 indicate that many teachers struggle to provide equitable, high-standard education due to inadequate classroom facilities. The lack of well-equipped and functional learning spaces in many schools limits the ability to conduct lessons aligned with the core content and learning objectives of the national curriculum, Lgr22. Insufficient resources not only restrict students' opportunities for hands-on learning but also compromise safety and the overall quality of instruction

The framework conditions for Home Economics studies are largely governed by national policies and legislation, including the Education Act, the Food Act, and the Work Environment Act. By aligning teaching practices with these regulations, schools can establish a foundation for safe, high quality, and legally compliant education. Home Economics should be taught in a way that supports students' learning, engagement, and well-being. In addition to physical resources, structural factors play a crucial role in shaping Home Economics education as a whole. Elements such as class size, the subject's placement in the timetable, the availability of sustainable schedules with subject-specific transition time, adequate time for classroom maintenance, and opportunities for professional development all influence the effectiveness of instruction.

Addressing these factors is essential for creating a supportive teaching environment where both educators and students can thrive.

The regulatory documents governing Home Economics studies play a crucial role in ensuring that the subject is conducted in a legally sound, pedagogically effective, and high-quality manner. These regulations provide a structured framework for teaching, ensuring that students acquire knowledge and skills that are both relevant and adapted to their needs. A key component of this framework is the Education Act, which mandates that teaching must be tailored to each student's individual needs and abilities. Given that Home Economics focuses on practical and everyday knowledge, it is essential that students have the opportunity to develop their skills based on their own experiences and circumstances. The Education Act also emphasises that education should be based on the best interests of the child and promote human rights. In Home Economics, this translates into equipping students with knowledge about healthy eating, personal finance, and sustainable consumption, enabling them to make informed decisions in their daily lives. Additionally, national guidelines for school meals serve as an important educational tool, helping students understand the relationship between proper nutrition and overall health.

Since Home Economics studies involves hands-on activities such as cooking, food handling, and kitchen work, workplace safety and environmental regulations are of central importance. The Work Environment Act and other safety regulations ensure a secure learning environment for both students and teachers. Implementing clear safety guidelines for working in Home Economics classrooms is essential to prevent accidents and injuries, particularly when using sharp tools, heat sources, and electrical appliances. Moreover, the physical environment must be carefully designed to be both safe and functional, allowing for efficient workflows, hygienic food preparation, and accessible learning spaces that accommodate all students. By adhering to these legal and pedagogical guidelines, schools can create a structured, engaging, and safe Home Economics learning environment - one that not only meets curriculum requirements but also equips students with practical life skills essential for their future well-being and independence.

Food legislation is a fundamental aspect of Home Economics studies, as students must learn proper food handling, storage, and kitchen hygiene to ensure food safety. One key component of this is the HACCP system (Hazard Analysis and Critical Control Points), a method used to identify and prevent risks in food preparation. Integrating HACCP principles into Home Economics studies helps students develop a critical understanding of food safety protocols, which are essential both in daily life and in professional food service settings. Beyond food safety, environmental legislation also plays a significant role in shaping Home Economics studies. The subject should provide students with insights into sustainable consumption, food waste reduction, and the environmental impact of food production. By exploring these topics, students gain awareness of how their choices - such as selecting locally produced, organic, or plant-based foods - can contribute to a more sustainable future. In addition, local policy documents, including public health plans and school meal policy programs, influence teaching by setting guidelines for how schools promote nutrition, well-being, and responsible consumption.

In addition to legal and pedagogical frameworks, risk assessment and safety protocols are critical in Home Economics studies. Since students work with hot surfaces, sharp tools, and electrical appliances, it is essential to identify, assess, and mitigate potential hazards. Special attention must be given to fire safety, as cooking activities naturally increase the risk of kitchen fires. Schools must also establish clear procedures for handling conflicts, preventing harassment, and addressing potential threats, as these factors directly influence the overall security and inclusivity of the learning environment.

Regulatory documents and safety measures play a crucial role in shaping a safe, equitable, and well-structured learning environment in Home Economics. They ensure that students not only acquire essential knowledge in nutrition, personal finance, and consumer awareness but also develop the ability to make responsible, informed decisions in their daily lives and within society.

Home Economics is more than just a practical subject: it equips students with the lifelong skills and awareness necessary for well-being, sustainability, and informed citizenship.

Referenser

Aléx, P. (2002). *Skolkökslärarinnorna och kunskapen om hemmet i sekelskiftets utmaningar.* I Essäer om välfärd, utbildning och nationell identitet vid sekelskiftet 1900 (s. xx–xx). Carlssons.

Andersson, J. (2014). *Kroppsliggörande, erfarenhet och pedagogiska processer*: En undersökning av lärande av kroppstekniker (Doktorsavhandling, Uppsala universitet).

Anttalainen, H., & Manninen, M. (2014). *Kotitalouden opetustilat ja työturvallisuus* (Oppaat ja käsikirjat 2013:10). Opetushallitus. https://www.oph.fi/sites/default/files/documents/kotitalouden_opetustila tjatyoturvallisuus0.pdf

Arbetsmiljöverket. (2012). *Belastningsergonomi: Arbetsmiljöverkets författningssamling* (AFS 2012:2). https://www.av.se/globalassets/filer/publikationer/foreskrifter/belastning sergonomi-foreskrifter-afs2012-2.pdf

Arbetsmiljöverket. (2013). *Om minderårigas arbetsmiljö: Vägledning till Arbetsmiljöverkets föreskrifter minderårigas arbetsmiljö* (AFS 2012:3). Lenanders Grafiska.

Arbetsmiljöverket. (2017). *Arbetsmiljön i skolan.* https://www.av.se/globalassets/filer/publikationer/broschyrer/arbetsmilj on-i-skolan-broschyr-adi565.pdf

Arbetsmiljöverket. (2018). *Smittrisker: Arbetsmiljöverkets föreskrifter och allmänna råd om smittrisker* (AFS 2018:4). https://www.av.se/globalassets/filer/publikationer/foreskrifter/smittriske r_afs_2018_4.pdf

Arbetsmiljöverket. (2020). *Bort med bullret i skolan.* https://www.av.se/globalassets/filer/publikationer/broschyrer/bort-med-bullret-i-skolan-affisch-adi608.pdf

Arbetsmiljöverket. (2023a). *Arbetsmiljöverkets föreskrifter och allmänna råd (AFS 2023:2) om planering och organisering av arbetsmiljöarbete – Grundläggande skyldigheter för dig med arbetsgivaransvar.* https://www.av.se/arbetsmiljoarbete-och-inspektioner/publikationer/foreskrifter/beslutade-foreskrifter-som-trader-i-kraft-2025/afs-20232/

Arbetsmiljöverket. (2023b). *Förebygg smittspridning i skolan.* https://www.av.se/halsa-och-sakerhet/sjukdomar-smitta-och-mikrobiologiska-risker/smittrisker-i-arbetsmiljon/forebyggande-atgarder-mot-smittrisker/att-tanka-pa-vid-atergang-till-skola/?hl=skola

Arbetsmiljöverket. (2024a). *Skyddsombud och arbetsmiljöombud.* https://www.av.se/arbetsmiljoarbete-och-inspektioner/skyddsombud-och-arbetsmiljoombud/

Arbetsmiljöverket. (2024b). *Buller från maskiner.* https://www.av.se/halsa-och-sakerhet/buller/forebyggande-om-buller/buller-fran-maskiner/

Beinert, C., Palojoki, P., Åbacka, G., Hardy-Johnson, P., Engeset, D., Hillesund, E. R., Selvik Ask, A. M., Øverby, N. C., & Vik, F. N. (2021). *The mismatch between teaching practices and curriculum goals in Norwegian home economics classes: A missed opportunity.* Education Inquiry, 12(2), 183–201. https://doi.org/10.1080/20004508.2020.1816677

Belasco, W. (2008). *Food: The key concepts.* Bloomsbury Publishing.

Belt, A. (2013). *Kun työrauha horjuu: Kotitalousopettajien käsityksiä työrauhahäiriöistä ja niiden taustatekijöistä* (Acta Universitatis Ouluensis E Scientiae Rerum Socialium, 135). Oulun Yliopistopaino. http://jultika.oulu.fi/files/isbn9789526202372.pdf

Bergström, G., & Bergström, M. (2013). Likvärdighet – perspektiv på tre olika nivåer. In O. Johansson & L. Svedberg (Red.), *Att leda mot skolans mål* (s. xx–xx). Gleerups Utbildning.

Blomhoff, R., Andersen, R., Arnesen, E. K., Christensen, J. J., Eneroth, H., Erkkola, M., Gudanaviciene, I., Halldorsson, T. I., Høyer-Lund, A., Lemming, E. W., Meltzer, H. M., Pitsi, T., Schwab, U., Siksna, I., Thorsdottir, I., & Trolle, E. (2023). *Nordic Nutrition Recommendations 2023*. Nordiska Ministerrådet.

Bohm, I. (2022). *"We can never close the book and say, 'We'll continue next week'" – The rhythms of cooking and learning to cook in Swedish home economics*. Food, Culture & Society, 25(3), 604–619. https://doi.org/10.1080/15528014.2021.2002057

Boverket. (2008). *Boverkets byggregler*, BBR 2008.

Boverket. (2023). *Krav på säkerhet i händelse av brand*. https://www.boverket.se/sv/PBL-kunskapsbanken/regler-om-byggande/boverkets-byggregler/brandskydd/

Boverket. (2024). *Bättre ljudklass än BBR*. https://www.boverket.se/sv/PBL-kunskapsbanken/regler-om-byggande/boverkets-byggregler/bullerskydd/ljudklassning/

Brandskyddsföreningen. (2023). *Skolan*. https://www.brandskyddsforeningen.se/brandsakerhet/skolan/

Britton, T., & Johansson, M. (2022). *Frågedriven undervisning – en planerings- och undervisningsmodell med ett exempel från religionskunskap*. SO-didaktik, 11, 8–19.

Brown, A. L., Bransford, J. D., Ferrara, R., & Campione, J. (1983). Learning, remembering, and understanding. I J. H. Flavell & E. M. Markman (Red.), *Handbook of child psychology: Vol. 3. Cognitive development* (4th ed., s. 77–166). Wiley.

Brown, A. L. (1997). *Transforming schools into communities of thinking and learning about serious matters*. American Psychologist, 52, 399–413.

Böhme, J., Walsh, Z., & Wamsler, C. (2022). *Sustainable lifestyles: Towards a relational approach.* Sustainability Science, 17, 2063–2076. https://doi.org/10.1007/s11625-022-01117-y

Cullbrand, I., & Petersson, M. (2005). *Nationella utvärderingen av grundskolan 2003 (NU-03): Hem- och konsumentkunskap.* Göteborgs universitet.

De Ron, L., & Feldt, M. (2013). *Lära och bedöma: I hem- och konsumentkunskap Lgr 11* (1 uppl.). Vulkan.
Derry, S., & Murphy, D. (1986). *Designing systems that train learning ability: From theory to practice.* Review of Educational Research, 56, 1–39.

European Food Safety Authority (EFSA). (2014). *Scientific opinion on the evaluation of allergenic foods and food ingredients for labelling purposes.* Parma, Italy. https://efsa.onlinelibrary.wiley.com/doi/epdf/10.2903/j.efsa.2014.3894

Enfield, R. P., Schmitt-McQuitty, L., & Smith, M. H. (2007). *The development and evaluation of experiential learning workshops for 4-H volunteers.* Journal of Extension, 45(1).

Eriksson, E. (1998). *Den moderna stadens födelse: Svensk arkitektur 1890–1920.* Ordfronts förlag.

EU-förordningen (EG) nr 852/2004. https://eur-lex.europa.eu/legal-content/SV/TXT/?uri=celex%3A32004R0852

EU-förordningen (EG) nr 853/2004. https://eur-lex.europa.eu/eli/reg/2004/853/oj/swe

EUR-Lex. (2016). *Försiktighetsprincipen: Artikel 191.* https://eur-lex.europa.eu/legal-content/SV/TXT/?uri=LEGISSUM:precautionary_principle

Folkhälsomyndigheten. (2022a). *Tillsynsvägledning om hälsoskydd i skolor och förskolor* (Artikel 22056). https://www.folkhalsomyndigheten.se/publikationer-och-material/publikationsarkiv/t/tillsynsvagledning-om-halsoskydd-i-skolor-och-forskolor/?pub=115733

Folkhälsomyndigheten. (2022b). *TILL DIG SOM DRIVER EN SKOLA ELLER FÖRSKOLA: Egenkontroll av inomhusmiljö i skolan och förskolan.* https://www.folkhalsomyndigheten.se/contentassets/c057f0fd48554faca c52c5f5013a9157/egenkontroll-av-inomhusmiljon-skolan-forskolan.pdf

Folkhälsomyndigheten. (2022c). *Hur hänger olika skolfaktorer samman med ungdomars hälsa och välbefinnande i Sverige?* Analyser på data från Skolbarns hälsovanor. Solna.

Folkhälsomyndigheten. (2022d). *På väg mot en god och jämlik hälsa: Stödstruktur för det statliga folkhälsoarbetet.* https://www.folkhalsomyndigheten.se/contentassets/bd19f6bb308043ed 9da8dfffcb3a5e67/stodstruktur-god-jamlik-halsa.pdf

Garner, R. (1990). *When children and adults do not use learning strategies: Towards a theory of settings.* Review of Educational Research, 60, 517–529.

Gelinder, L. (2020). *Smak för hållbar mat? Undervisning för hållbar matkonsumtion i Hem- och konsumentkunskap* (Doktorsavhandling, Uppsala universitet).

Gelinder, L. (2024). *Att utveckla smak för hållbarhet. Del 4: Smak för hållbarhet,* Skolverkets Modul: Undervisning i hem- och konsumentkunskap. Skolverket, Läroportalen.

Gustafsson, I-B., Öström, Å., Johansson, J., & Mossberg, L. (2006). *The Five Aspects Meal Model: A tool for developing meal services in restaurants.* Journal of Foodservice, 17(2), 65–76.

Gustafsson, J-E., Allodi Westling, M., Åkerman, A., Eriksson, C., Eriksson, L., Fischbein, S., et al. (2010). *School, learning and mental health: A systematic review.* Stockholm: The Royal Academy of Sciences, The Health Committee.

Halås, C. T., & Fuglseth, K. S. (2023). *En kort introduktion till ämnet praktisk kunskap*. In K. S. Torbjörnsen & C. T. Halås (Red.), Praktisk kunskap – en introduktion (1:a uppl., s. 9–16). Gleerups.

Hattie, J. (2009). *Visible learning: A synthesis of over 800 meta-analyses relating to achievement*. Routledge.

Hattie, J. (2014a). *Synligt lärande: En syntes av mer än 800 metaanalyser om vad som påverkar elevers skolresultat* (1:a uppl.). Natur & Kultur.

Hattie, J., & Yates, G. (2014b). *Hur vi lär: Synligt lärande och vetenskapen om våra lärprocesser.* Natur & Kultur.

Hjälmeskog, K. (Red.). (2006). *Lärarprofession i förändring: Från "skolkök" till hem- och konsumentkunskap*. Föreningen för svensk undervisningshistoria.

Holmberg, U., Johansson, P., Britton, T. H., Johansson, M., & Nordgren, K. (2022). *Frågedriven undervisning för att organisera normativa kunskapspraktiker i SO-ämnena*. Nordidactica, 12(4), 124–153.

Hjälmeskog, K. (2024). *Bortom normativ undervisning – hållbar utveckling i hem- och konsumentkunskap. Del 3: Bortom normativ undervisning,* Skolverkets Modul: Undervisning i hem- och konsumentkunskap. Skolverket, Läroportalen.

Höijer, K. (2024). *Kunskapssyn och bedömning i hem- och konsumentkunskap. Del 1: Kunskapssyn och bedömning,* Skolverkets Modul: Undervisning i hem- och konsumentkunskap. Skolverket, Läroportalen.

Højlund, S. (2020). *Figurations of taste: Sensing sustainable alternatives together*. International Journal of Food Design, 5(1–2), 133–138. https://doi.org/10.1386/ijfd_00016_3

Katrineholms Kommun. (2024). *Hållbara måltider ger matglädje genom livet: Måltidspolitiskt program 2024–2027*. Katrineholms

kommun.
https://www.katrineholm.se/download/18.16fc068e18d2a6eb1ce12d31/
1706166970478/M%C3%A5ltidspolitiskt%20program%202024%20-
%202027,%20KF%202024-01-15%20%C2%A7%205.pdf

Kemikalieinspektionen. (2011). *Kemikalier i varor - strategier &
styrmedel för att minska risker med farliga ämnen i vardagen* (Rapport
nr 3/2011).

Kemikalieinspektionen. (2024). *Färger och lacker - VOC-direktivet.*
https://www.kemi.se/lagar-och-regler/lagstiftningar-inom-
kemikalieomradet/eu-gemensam-lagstiftning/farger-och-lacker---voc

Kronofogden. (2022). *Unga har allt större skulder hos Kronofogden.*
https://kronofogden.se/om-kronofogden/analyser/skuldsattning-
blandunga-vuxna

Larsson, E. (2008). *Naiseuden monet muodot* [Licentiat Avhandling].
Turku University.

Larsson, E. (2011). *Kotikuvauksen ideaalisuus Carl Larssonin
teoksessa Ett hem (1899)* [Doctorssvhandling]. Turku University. ISBN
978-951-29-4548-1.

Larsson, E. (2024). *Matarbete i grupp* [Intervju]. Skolverket.
https://larportalen.skolverket.se/moduler/M942/2

Lind, J. (2016). *Likvärdig bedömning utan likvärdiga förutsättningar?
Hem- och konsumentkunskap som exempel.*
https://gupea.ub.gu.se/bitstream/2077/43412/1/gupea_2077_43412_1.p
df

Lindblom, C. (2016). *Skolämnet Hem- och konsumentkunskap på 2000-
talet – förutsättningar för elevers möjlighet till måluppfyllelse.*
Institutionen för kostvetenskap, Umeå Universitet.
https://www.skolporten.se/app/uploads/2016/05/fulltext01-12.pdf

Lindblom, C., Erixon Arreman, I., & Hörnell, A. (2013). *Practical
conditions for Home and Consumer Studies in Swedish compulsory*

education: A survey study. International Journal of Consumer Studies, 37, 556–563. https://doi.org/10.1111/ijcs.12027

Lindblom, C. (2024). *Grupparbete i hem- och konsumentkunskap. Del 2: Grupparbete*, Skolverkets Modul: Undervisning i hem- och konsumentkunskap. Skolverket, Läroportalen.

Livsmedelsverket. (2010). *Bra mat i förskolan 2010*. Uppsala.

Livsmedelsverket. (2018). *Riksmaten ungdom 2016-17, Livsmedelskonsumtion bland ungdomar i Sverige*. https://www.livsmedelsverket.se/globalassets/publikationsdatabas/rappo rter/2018/2018-nr-14-riksmatenungdom-huvudrapport_del-1-livsmedelskonsumtion.pdf

Livsmedelsverket. (2019). *Nationella riktlinjer för måltider i skolan - Förskoleklass, grundskola, gymnasieskola och fritidshem*. Uppsala. ISBN: 978-91-7714-266-9. https://www.livsmedelsverket.se/globalassets/publikationsdatabas/brosc hyrer-foldrar/riktlinjer-for-maltider-i-skolan.pdf

Livsmedelsverket. (2021a). *Nationella riktlinjer för måltider i skolan*. https://www.livsmedelsverket.se/globalassets/publikationsdatabas/brosc hyrer-foldrar/riktlinjer-for-maltider-i-skolan.pdf

Livsmedelsverket. (2021b). *Lokaler, hygien och företagens egen kontroll*. https://www.livsmedelsverket.se/foretagande-regler-kontroll/regler-for-livsmedelsforetag/lokaler_hygien_foretagens_egen_kontroll

Livsmedelsverket. (2023a). *Måltidsmodellen*. https://www.livsmedelsverket.se/matvanor-halsa--miljo/maltider-i-vard-skola-och-omsorg/maltidsmodellen

Livsmedelsverket. (2023b). *Kontaktmaterial (material som kommer i kontakt med mat och dryck)*. https://www.livsmedelsverket.se/foretagande-regler-kontroll/regler-for-livsmedelsforetag/material-i-kontakt-med-livsmedel

Livsmedelsverket. (2023c). *Allergener - att tänka på för företag.*
https://www.livsmedelsverket.se/foretagande-regler-kontroll/regler-for-livsmedelsforetag/allergener#Symtom_p%C3%A5_matallergi
Livsmedelsverkets föreskrifter (SLVFS). (2001). *Hygienregler för livsmedelsanläggningar* (SLVFS 2001:30).

Livsmedelsverkets föreskrifter (SLVFS). (2006). *Livsmedelshygien, HACCP och egenkontroll* (SLVFS 2006:27).

LO, Lärarförbundet, Lärarnas Riksförbund. (2017). *Likvärdighetsagendan. Ge alla elever samma chans.* https://www.lr.se/download/18.2c5a365d1645ac11059e094/155902816 7923/Likvardighetsagendan_201701_v4.pdf

Lundgren, U. (1999). *Ramfaktorteori och praktisk utbildningsplanering.* Pedagogisk Forskning i Sverige, 4(1), 31–41. https://doi.org/10.16993/pfs.142

Lärarnas historia. (2024). TAM–arkivet. https://lararnashistoria.se/hushallslararnas-riksforenings-historia/

Mattanken. (2024). *Sammanställning av måltidspolicyer.* https://www.landsbygdsnatverket.se/mattanken/laravandra/samladkunsk apochmaterial/material/sammanstallningavmaltidspolicyer.5.237fd4c51 61a8ddde58df227.html

McGuirk, J. (2023a). *Den kloka praktikern.* In K. S. Torbjörnsen & C. T. Halås (Red.), Praktisk kunskap – en introduktion (s. 45–56). Gleerups.

McGuirk, J. (2023b). *Tyst kunskap.* In K. S. Torbjörnsen & C. T. Halås (Red.), Praktisk kunskap - en introduktion (s. 57–68). Gleerups.

Modin, R., & Lindblad, M. (2011). *Förvara maten rätt så håller den längre - vetenskapligt underlag om optimal förvaring av livsmedel.* Livsmedelsverkets rapportserie nr 20/2011.

Molander, B. (1996). *Kunskap i handling* (2 uppl.). Daidalos.

Myndigheten för samhällsskydd och beredskap. (2022). *Brandskydd i byggnader och anläggningar.*
https://www.msb.se/sv/amnesomraden/skydd-mot-olyckor-och-farliga-amnen/brandskydd/brandskydd-i-byggnader-och-anlaggningar/

Myndigheten för samhällsskydd och beredskap. (2024). *Vägledning – samverkan vid pågående dödligt våld i publik miljö.*
https://rib.msb.se/filer/pdf/28461.pdf

Newsham, G., Brand, J., Donnelly, C., Veitch, J., Aries, M., & Charles, K. (2009). *Linking indoor environment conditions to job satisfaction: A field study.* Building Research & Information, 37(2), 129–147.
https://doi.org/10.1080/09613210802710298

Nylander, L. (2020). *Lugn och ro bristvara i skolan.* Forskning.se.
https://www.forskning.se/2020/08/20/lugn-och-ro-bristvara-i-skolan/#

Ojala, M. (2016). *Facing anxiety in climate change education: From therapeutic practice to hopeful transgressive learning.* Canadian Journal of Environmental Education, 21, 41–56.

Olsson, E. (2021). *9 av 10 lärare stressas av kraven på dokumentation.* Vi lärare. https://www.vilarare.se/nyheter/arbetsmiljo/sa-fortsatter-dokumentationsmonstret-vaxa/

Olsson, E. (2024). *Hemkunskapen bantas – minimalt med matlagning.* Vi lärare.
https://www.vilarare.se/nyheter/nedskarningar/hemkunskapen-bantas--minimalt-med-matlagning/

Persson, L. (2016). *Health promotion in schools - Results of a Swedish public health project* (Karlstad University Studies | 2016:24). Karlstad University. http://kau.diva-portal.org/smash/get/diva2:916794/FULLTEXT02.pdf

Polisen. (2025). *Skolskjutningen i Örebro.*
https://polisen.se/aktuellt/skolskjutningen-i-orebro/

Rauste-von Wright, M. (1997). *Opettaja tienhaarassa - konstruktivismia käytännössä.* WSOY.

Rauste-von Wright, M., von Wright, J., & Soini, T. (2003). *Oppiminen ja koulutus.* WSOY.

Regeringen. (2009). *Regeringens proposition. Den nya skollagen – för kunskap, valfrihet och trygghet* (Diarienummer 2009/10:165). Regeringen. https://www.regeringen.se/contentassets/c507a849c3fa4173b7d03df20b ad2b59/den-nya-skollagen---for-kunskap-valfrihet-och-trygghet-hela-dokumentet-prop.-20092010165

Regeringen. (2017). *Samling för skolan: Nationell strategi för kunskap och likvärdighet* (SOU 2017:35). *Slutbetänkande av 2015 års skolkommission.* https://www.regeringen.se/498092/contentassets/e94a1c61289142bfbcf df54a44377507/samling-for-skolan---nationell-strategi-for-kunskap-och-likvardighet-sou-201735.pdf

Regeringen. (2025). *Tid för undervisningsuppdraget – åtgärder för god undervisning och läraryrkenas attraktivitet* (SOU 2025:26). Ministry of Education and Research. https://www.regeringen.se/rattsliga-dokument/statens-offentliga-utredningar/2025/03/sou-202526/ PDF version: https://www.regeringen.se/contentassets/6dfbf9bb877b433bbca46ad8c0 7950fe/tid-for-undervisningsuppdraget--atgarder-for-god-undervisning-och-lararyrkenas-attraktivitet-sou-202526.pdf

Regeringskansliet. (2020*). Remiss SOU 2020:28 En mer likvärdig skola – minskad skolsegregation och förbättrad resurstilldelning* (Diarienummer U2020/02667/S). Regeringskansliet. https://www.regeringen.se/remisser/2020/06/remiss-sou-202028-en-mer-likvardig-skola--minskad-skolsegregation-och-forbattrad-resurstilldelning/

Regeringskansliet. (2023). *En minskad administrativ börda för förskollärare och lärare* Diarienummer: 2023:72.

https://www.regeringen.se/rattsliga-dokument/kommittedirektiv/2023/06/dir.-202372

Regeringskansliet. (2024). *Elevers tillgång till läroböcker stärks. Pressmeddelande.* Publicerad 13 maj 2024. https://www.regeringen.se/pressmeddelanden/2024/05/elevers-tillgang-till-larobocker-starks/

Scheutz, S. (2017). *Likvärdig utbildning.* Iustus Förlag. Schmidt, C. V., & Mouritsen, O. (2020). *The solution to sustainable eating is not a one-way street. Frontiers in Psychology, 11.* https://doi.org/10.3389/fpsyg.2020.00531

Sigtuna Kommun. (2018). *Program för måltidsverksamheten i Sigtuna kommun.* https://www.sigtuna.se/download/18.6299176c16d2029d53130c0/1568366292492/Program%20f%C3%B6r%20m%C3%A5ltidsverksamheten%20i%20Sigtuna%20kommun.pdf

Skolinspektionen. (2019). *Hem- och Konsumentkunskap i årskurs 7–9: Tematisk kvalitetsgranskning 2019* (Diarienummer: 400-2017:7330). https://file:///C:/Users/elilar3/Downloads/hem-och-konsumentkunskap-i-ak-7-9.pdf

Skolverket. (2000). *Kommentarer till kursplaner och betygskriterier 2000.* Fritzes.

Skolverket. (2004). *Nationella utvärderingen av grundskolan 2003: Huvudrapport – bild, hem- och konsumentkunskap, idrott och hälsa, musik och slöjd* (NU03) (Rapport 253). Skolverket. https://www.skolverket.se/download/18.6bfaca41169863e6a6553a9/1553958486004/pdf1385.pdf

Skolverket. (2019*). Systematiskt kvalitetsarbete – så fungerar det.* https://www.skolverket.se/skolutveckling/leda-och-organisera-skolan/systematisktkvalitetsarbete-i-skola-och-forskola/systematiskt-kvalitetsarbete-i-skola-och-forskola

Skolverket. (2022). *Läroplan för Hem- och konsumentkunskap.*
https://www.skolverket.se/undervisning/grundskolan/laroplan-och-kursplaner-for-grundskolan/laroplan-Lgr22-for-grundskolan-samt-for-forskoleklassen-och-fritidshemmet?url=-996270488%2Fcompulsorycw%2Fjsp%2Fsubject.htm%3FsubjectCode%3DGRGRHKK01%26tos%3DDgr&sv.url=12.5dfee44715d35a5cdfa219f

Skolverket. (2022). *Kommentarer till allmänna råd för arbete med extra anpassningar, särskilt stöd och åtgärdsprogram.*
https://www.skolverket.se/getFile?file=10021

Skolverket. (2024a). *Timplan för grundskolan.*
https://www.skolverket.se/undervisning/grundskolan/laroplan-och-kursplaner-for-grundskolan/timplan-for-grundskolan

Skolverket. (2024b). *Lärportalen, Moduler för hem- och konsumentkunskap.* https://larportalen.skolverket.se/moduler/M942

Sonmark, K., & Modin, B. (2017). Psychosocial work environment in school and students' somatic health complaints: An analysis of buffering resources. *Scandinavian Journal of Public Health*, 45(1), 64–72.

SOU 2020:28. (2020). *Utredningen om en mer likvärdig skola: En mer likvärdig skola – minskad skolsegregation och förbättrad resurstilldelning.*

Sporre, K., & Osbeck, C. (2022). Responding to Voices of Children. I H. Lotz-Sisitka & E. Rosenberg (Red.), *Education in times of climate change* (s. 96–99). Rhodes University.
http://urn.kb.se/resolve?urn=urn:nbn:se:umu:diva-200157

Strömstad Kommun. (2022). *Kostpolicy.*
https://www.stromstad.se/download/18.fc6ae6c153c5fdf8ad116b6/1674027226947/Kostpolicy%20Str%C3%B6mstad.pdf

Svenaeus, F. (2009). Vad är praktisk kunskap? En inledning till ämnet och boken. I J. Bornemark & F. Svenaeus (Red.), *Vad är praktisk kunskap?* (s. 11–34). Södertörns högskola.

Svedberg, O. (2001). *Arkitekternas Århundrade: Europas arkitektur 1800-talet.* Arkitektur, Stockholm.

Svenska Arbetsmiljöverkets Föreskrifter (AFS 2020:1). (2020). *Arbetsplatsens utformning.* Arbetsmiljöverket.
https://www.av.se/globalassets/filer/publikationer/foreskrifter/arbetsplatsens-utformning-afs2020-1.pdf
Svenska Institutet för Standarder. (2023*). Byggnadsakustik – Ljudkrav för utrymmen i byggnader – Vårdlokaler, undervisningslokaler, förskolor och fritidshem, kontor, hotell och restauranger.* SVENSK STANDARD · SS 25268:2023.

Svensk författningssamling. (1949). *Föräldrabalk* (SFS 1949:381).
https://www.riksdagen.se/sv/dokument-och-lagar/dokument/svensk-forfattningssamling/foraldrabalk-1949381_sfs-1949-381/

Svensk författningssamling. (1977). *Arbetsmiljölag* (SFS 1977:1160).
https://www.riksdagen.se/sv/dokument-och-lagar/dokument/svensk-forfattningssamling/arbetsmiljolag-19771160_sfs-1977-1160/

Svensk Författningssamling. (1982). *Arbetstidslag* (SFS 1982:673).
https://www.riksdagen.se/sv/dokument-och-lagar/dokument/svensk-forfattningssamling/arbetstidslag-1982673_sfs-1982-673/

Svensk Författningssamling. (1998). *Miljöbalk* (SFS 1998:808).
https://www.riksdagen.se/sv/dokument-och-lagar/dokument/svensk-forfattningssamling/miljobalk-1998808_sfs-1998-808/

Svensk Författningssamling. (2003*). Lag om skydd mot olyckor* (SFS 2003:778). https://www.riksdagen.se/sv/dokument-och-lagar/dokument/svensk-forfattningssamling/lag-2003778-om-skydd-mot-olyckor_sfs-2003-778/

Svensk författningssamling. (2006). *Livsmedelslagen* (SFS 2006:804).
https://www.riksdagen.se/sv/dokument-och-lagar/dokument/svensk-forfattningssamling/livsmedelslag-2006804_sfs-2006-804/

Svensk Författningssamling. (2008). *Diskrimineringslag* (SFS 2008:567). https://www.riksdagen.se/sv/dokument-och-lagar/dokument/svensk-forfattningssamling/diskrimineringslag-2008567_sfs-2008-567/

Svensk Författningssamling. (2010). *Skollagen* (SFS 2010:800). https://www.riksdagen.se/sv/dokument-lagar/dokument/svensk-forfattningssamling/skollag2010800_sfs-2010-800

Svensk Författningssamling. (2010). *Plan- och bygglag* (SFS 2010:900). https://www.riksdagen.se/sv/dokument-och-lagar/dokument/svensk-forfattningssamling/plan-och-bygglag-2010900_sfs-2010-900/

Svensk Författningssamling. (2011). *Plan- och byggförordning* (SFS 2011:338). https://www.riksdagen.se/sv/dokument-och-lagar/dokument/svensk-forfattningssamling/plan-och-byggforordning-2011338_sfs-2011-338/

Svensk Författningssamling. (2011). *Skolförordningen* (SFS 2011:185). https://lagen.nu/2011:185

Svensk Författningssamling. (2018). *Lag om brandskydd* (SFS 2018:208). https://www.riksdagen.se/sv/dokument-och-lagar/dokument/svensk-forfattningssamling/lag-2018218-med-kompletterande-bestammelser_sfs-2018-218/

Sveriges Kommuner och Regioner. (2024). *Offentlig säker mat.* https://skr.se/offentligsakermat.32844.html

Sveriges Lärare. (2023). *Grupp- och klasstorlekar, extra anpassningar och särskilt stöd i skolformerna förskoleklass till komvux* (Statistiskt faktablad 2023:2). Sveriges Lärare. https://media.tmkontor.se/SVLT1071--SVLSF23-2-Gruppstorlekar-extra-anpassningar-och-sarskilt-stod-fran-forskoleklass-till-komvux-230621.pdf

Sveriges Regering. (2020*). Utredningen om en mer likvärdig skola: En mer likvärdig skola: minskad skolsegregation och förbättrad resurstilldelning* (SOU 2020:28). https://www.regeringen.se/contentassets/fcf0e59defe04870a39239f5bda

331f4/en-mer-likvardig-skola--minskad-skolsegregation-och-forbattrad-resurstilldelning-sou-202028/

Taylor, L., Watkins, S. L., Marshall, H., Dascombe, B. J., & Foster, J. (2016). *The impact of different environmental conditions on cognitive function: A focused review.* Frontiers in Physiology, 6, 372. https://doi.org/10.3389/fphys.2015.00372
Turunen, M., Toyinbo, O., Putus, T., Nevalainen, A., Shaughnessy, R., & Haverinen-Shaughnessy, U. (2014). *Indoor environmental quality in school buildings, and the health and wellbeing of students.* International Journal of Hygiene and Environmental Health, 217(7), 733–739.

Tynjälä, P. (1999). *Oppiminen tiedon rakentamisena: Konstruktivistisen oppimiskäsityksen perusteita.* Tammer-Paino Oy.

Ung privatekonomi. (2021). *Ungdomar vill ha mer privatekonomi i skolan.*

Unicef. (2018). *An unfair start: Inequality in children's education in rich countries.* https://blog.unicef.se/2018/10/30/sverige-brister-nar-det-galler-likvardighet-i-skolan/

United Nations (UN). (2022). *Sustainable Development Goals.* https://www.un.org/sustainabledevelopment/sustainable-consumption-production/

Willett, W., Rockström, J., Loken, B., et al. (2019). *Food in the Anthropocene: The 12 (12) EAT–Lancet Commission on healthy diets from sustainable food systems.* The Lancet, 393(10170), 447–492.

Examples of Different Design Plans
for a Home Economics Classroom I

An inspirational design plan for a Home Economics classroom.
By E. Larsson, created with the help of a graphic design program and Ikea's planning tool.

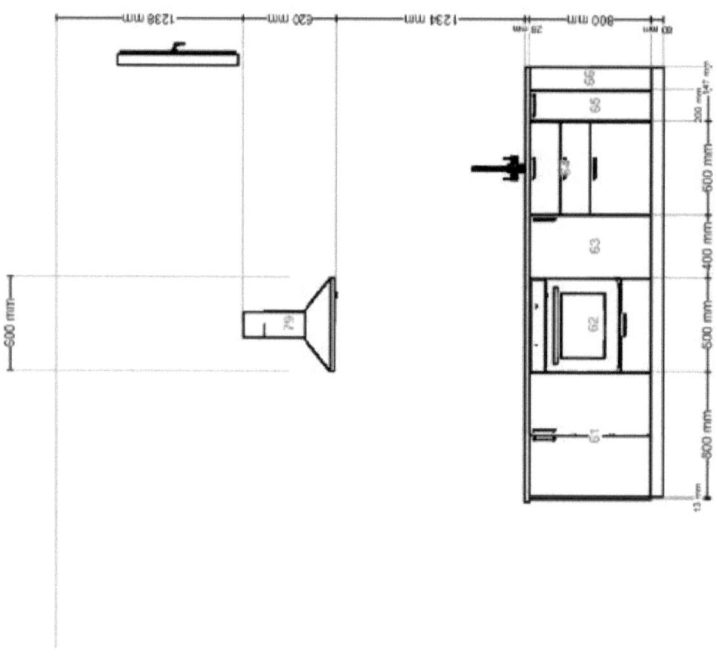

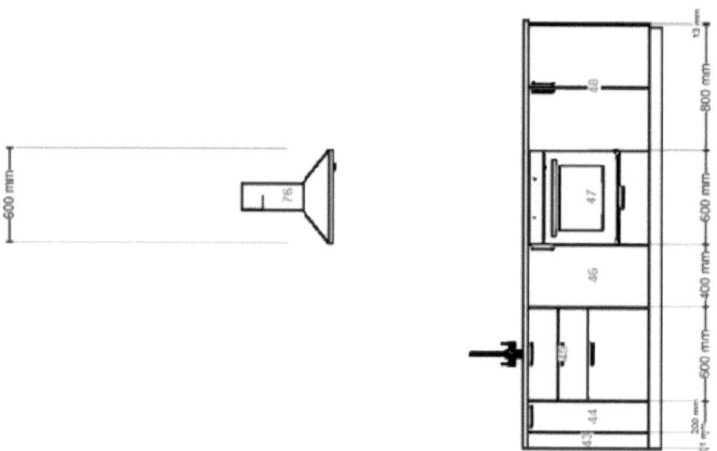

An inspirational design plan for a Home Economics classroom.
By E. Larsson, created with the help of a graphic design program and Ikea's planning tool.

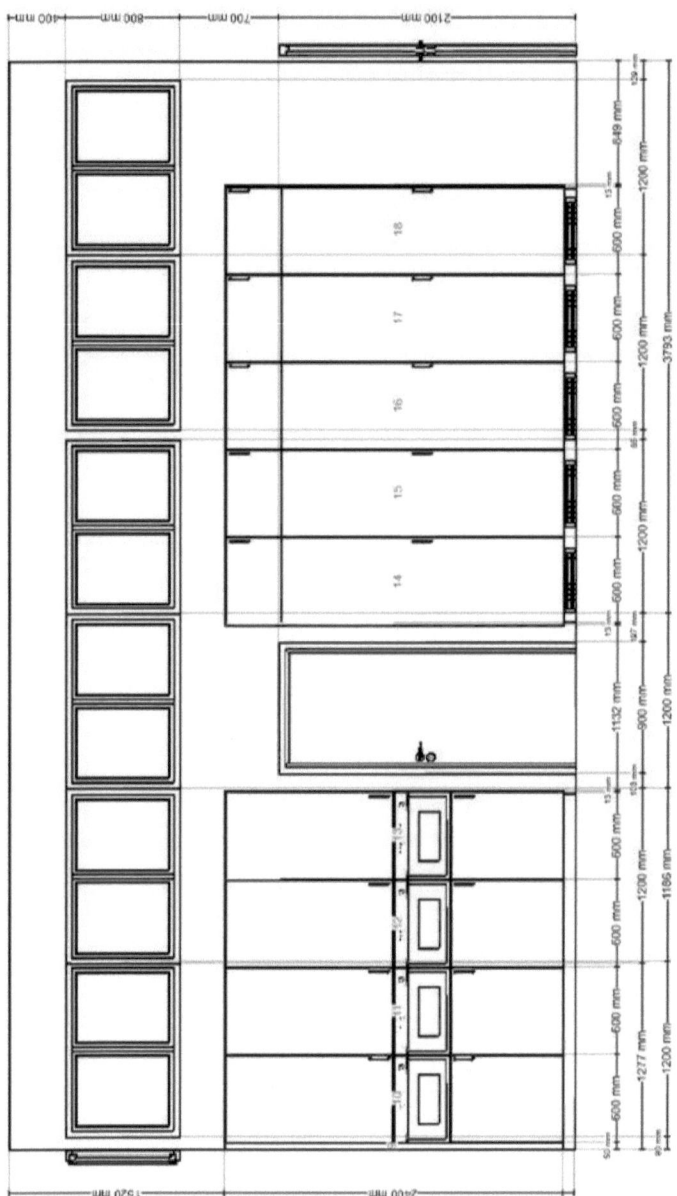

An inspirational design plan for a Home Economics classroom.
By E. Larsson, created with the help of a graphic design program and Ikea's planning tool.

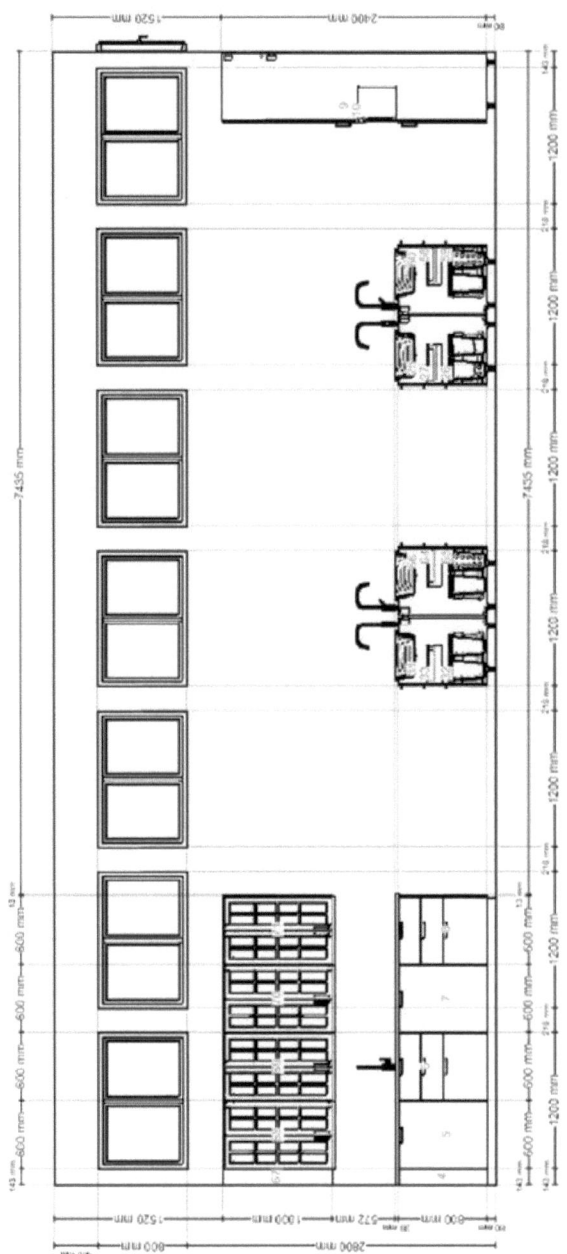

An inspirational design plan for a Home Economics classroom.
By E. Larsson, created with the help of a graphic design program and Ikea's planning tool.

An inspirational design plan for a Home Economics classroom.
By E. Larsson, created with the help of a graphic design program and Ikea's planning tool.

Examples of Different Design Plans
for a Home Economics Classroom II

An inspirational design plan for a Home Economics classroom.
By E. Larsson, created with the help of a graphic design program and Ikea's planning tool.

DESIGN FOR OPTIMAL CLASSROOM SETTINGS
By Elina Larsson

An inspirational design plan for a Home Economics classroom.
By E. Larsson, created with the help of a graphic design program and Ikea's planning tool.

HOME-ECONOMICS CLASSROOM

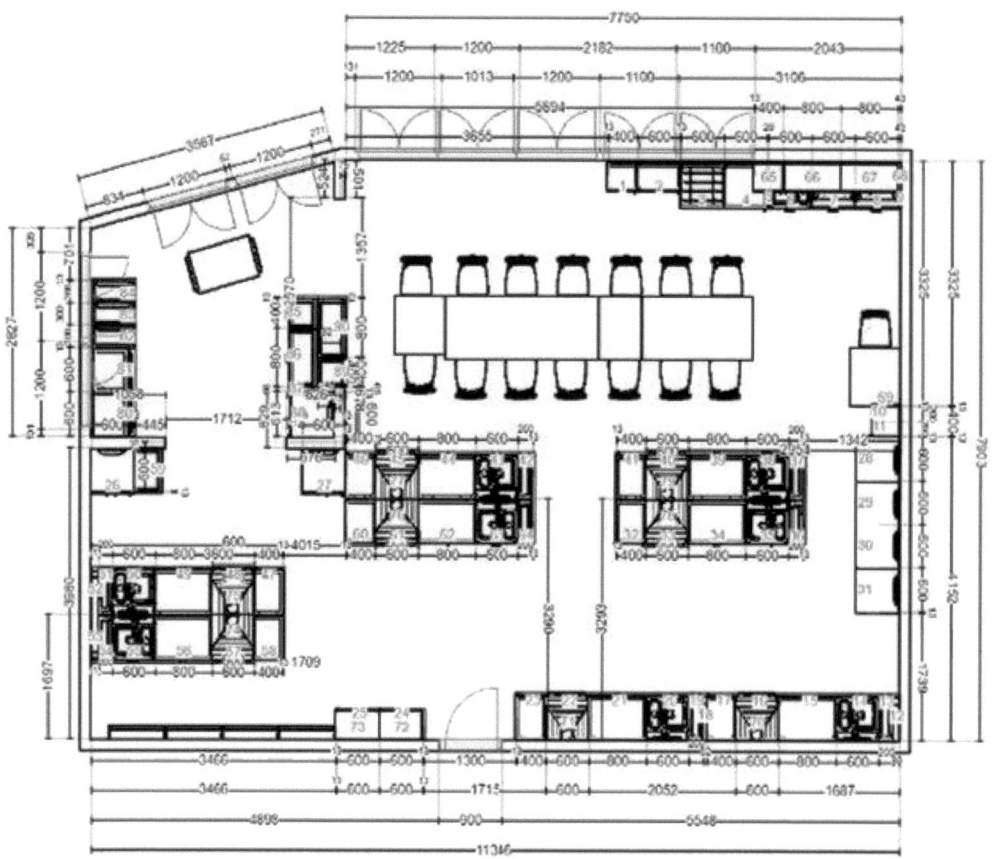

DESIGN FOR OPTIMAL CLASSROOM SETTINGS

By Elina Larsson

An inspirational design plan for a Home Economics classroom.
By E. Larsson, created with the help of a graphic design program and Ikea's planning tool.

Home Economics Classroom

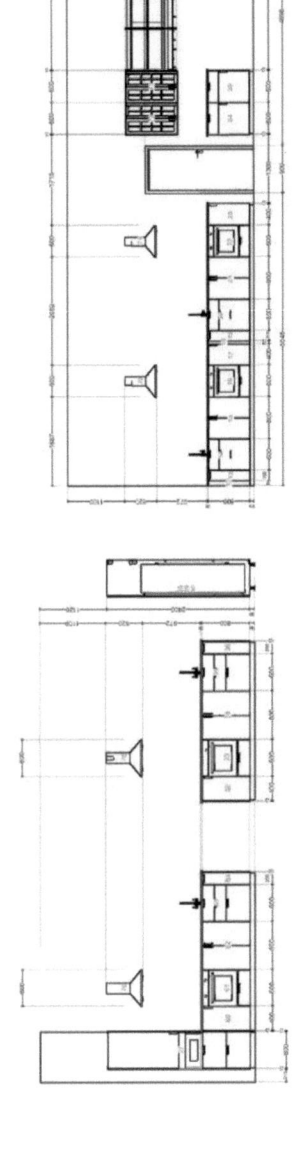

DESIGN FOR OPTIMAL CLASSROOM SETTINGS

By Elina Larsson

An inspirational design plan for a Home Economics classroom.

By E. Larsson, created with the help of a graphic design program and Ikea's planning tool.

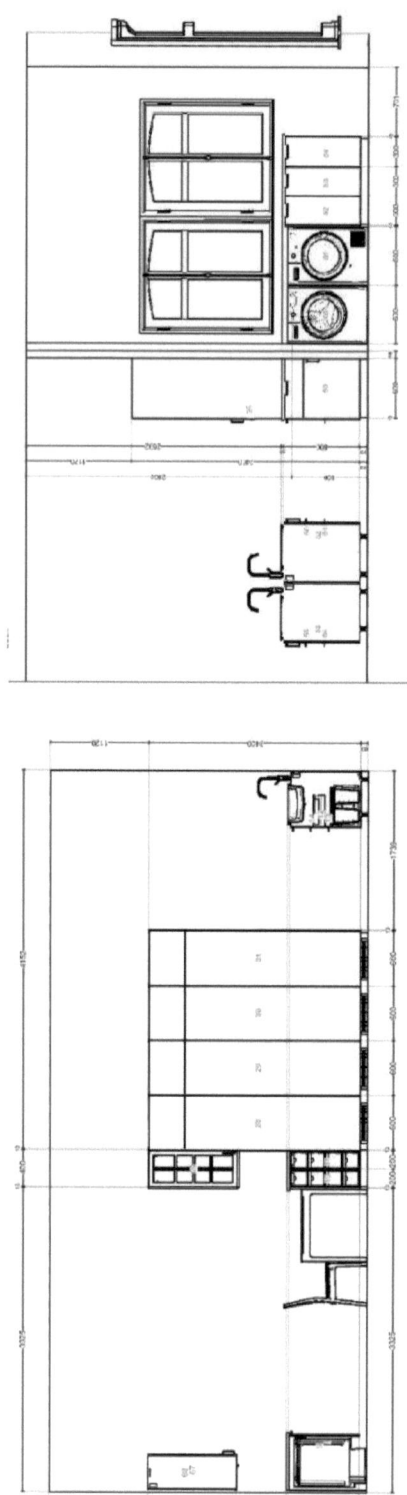

DESIGN FOR OPTIMAL CLASSROOM SETTINGS

By Elina Larsson

An inspirational design plan for a Home Economics classroom.

By E. Larsson, created with the help of a graphic design program and Ikea's planning tool.